PROTECTING HUMAN RIGHTS
Role of State Human Rights Commissions in Northeast India

Protecting Human Rights

Role of State Human Rights Commissions in Northeast India

Anuj Kanchan Datta Roy

AKANSHA PUBLISHING HOUSE
NEW DELHI • GUWAHATI • VISAKHAPATNAM

AKANSHA PUBLISHING HOUSE
4649-B/21, Ansari Road
Daryaganj, New Delhi-110002
Phones: 23268193, 09435116718
Email: ektabooks@yahoo.com
visit us: www.akanshapublishinghouse.com

Protecting Human Rights: Role of State Human Rights Commissions in Northeast India

First Published 2011

ISBN 978-81-8370-273-7

PRINTED IN INDIA

Published by Akansha Publishing House, New Delhi-110002 and printed at Harmain Offset Printers, Delhi.

'Baba', 'Maa' & Rup

Contents

Foreword

In India inclusion of civil, political and socio-economic and cultural rights in the Constitution and adoption of the Protection of Human Rights Act, 1993 have been the important landmarks in the development and guarantee of human rights.

The Constitution of National Human Rights Commission with its counterpart in the states as State Human Rights Commission further strengthens the human rights regime. In addition to these, there are several enactments designed to protect the rights of vulnerable groups.

The North East India, though the name may suggest a composite geographical entity, consists of numerous cultural groups with distinct histories of their own, numerical strength and level of development. Besides being unique in terms of cultural, social and political heritage and diversity, it is also a region beset with problems. The various autonomy movements as also the actions of the government machineries have dislocated life of the common people for a long time. Needless to say, the guarantee of human rights of the people has become the casualty. There has been a long-standing demand by the different groups for the abolition of Armed Forces Special Power Act, 1958. The language of protest has been different in different times for the protection of the rights of the people. Apart from this, the low level of development and economic deprivation results in the denial of the basic social and economic rights guaranteed in the Constitution. This brings into focus the role of state agencies in ensuring the rights to the people.

Interestingly, only two states, Assam and Manipur have so far established the State Human Rights Commission. The author, Shri Anuj Kanchan Datta Roy has made a detailed study of the working of these institutions since their establishment and provide us an in depth analysis of their role in safeguarding the rights of the people.

Another important dimension of the study is the interface between the Commission and the NGOs. It examines not only the collaboration between these organizations but also examines the perception of the NGOs regarding the functioning of the Commissions.

These institutions have been established with the avowed objective of safeguarding the rights of people and to provide relief and redress as and when their rights are violated. However the study shows that after the initial enthusiasm there has been a steady decline in the registration of cases by the public. This implies that the Commission has not been able to generate sufficient awareness about its functioning among the people. Moreover the inability of the government to appoint regular chairperson and members has added to the problems of the Commissions.

This study throws important light on the structure and working of these institutions in comparative perspectives. In fact, no thorough work has so far been published on this important aspect of human rights protection in North East India. Hence the author's contribution to our understanding of the role of State Human Rights Commission is immense and laudable.

Professor Ranju R. Dhamala

Department of Political Science
Assam University
Silchar

Acknowledgements

First of all I am acknowledging Prof. Ranju R. Dhamala who has guided me, with heartiest thanks and deep sense of gratitude for her kind support since my days of M.A., to complete my entire work. Although her support is beyond acknowledgement. Her constant inspiration, supervision, esteemed guidance and valuable advice and constructive criticisms in carrying out my work is undeniable. It is not possible for me to express her support by writing few words.

I am extremely grateful to my teachers Prof. Debashish Bhattacharjee, Prof. Tanmoy Bhattacharjee, Mr. P. Kanaka Rao, Dr. Harsha S., and other faculty members of the Department of Political Science, Assam University for their support and necessary guidance from time to time.

I am also thankful to Dr. Chandrika Basu Majumder of Department of Political Science, Tripura University and Dr. Suparna Bhattacharya of North East Hill University, Shillong for their constant support. I am thankful to Prof. Ksh. Bimola Devi, Dr Senjam Mangi Singh and Dr. Dhanabir Laishram of Deparment of Political Science, Manipur University for their constant support, for providing me various literatures, advice and cooperation to carryout the work.

I immensely express my gratitude to the Chairperson, Members and Staff of AHRC & MHRC. My special thanks goes to Mr. Jyoti Tapan Barua of AHRC and Shri Y. Rameshchandra Singh, Deputy Secretary of MHRC for their help and cooperation.

I sincerely acknowledge the support and cooperation of Mahuya and Monoj. I am also thankful to Nilanjan, Kirit, Raju and Bikash for their time to time support.

I thank my uncle Shri Dhruba Brata Datta Roy, my aunty Smt Subrata Datta Roy and my sisters and brother for their moral support to carry out the entire work.

I extend my profound thankfulness to my mother Smt Sreeparna Datta Roy and my brother Shri Ayan Kanchan Datta Roy (Rup) without whose support the work may not be completed. I am acknowledging their constant support that I received not only in this work but in my entire life.

Last but not the least the person who is beyond acknowledgement, whenever I face any troubles I find him just with me; no matter how far he is, he is always with me in entire zigzag life of mine, and he is my father Sri Abhra Brata Datta Roy.

Finally, I am fully responsible in case of any mistakes in the book and none of the individuals mentioned above are responsible for the opinion expressed in the book.

Anuj Kanchan Datta Roy

Preface

Struggle for human rights has been remained a continuous process since the inception of humanity on this earth. The journey of human life from the state of nature to the present state of society has been marked by various urge for the protection of people's rights. To salute this fight, mankind adopted a number of documents both at international and national level. In India the Protection of Human Rights Act, 1993 is the basic document in this regard. Part III and V of this document deals with National Human Rights Commission (NHRC) and State Human Rights Commission (SHRC) respectively which are the fundamental state mechanisms to protect and promote human rights. A number of works so far has been done on NHRC, but this is for the first time that the present work attempts to take the reader, into the pros and cons of the role of State Human Rights Commissions in insurgent prone North East India.

In North East India SHRCs have been established only in two states—Assam and Manipur. The role of Assam Human Rights Commission and Manipur Human Rights Commission are examined against the functions as laid down in section 12 of the Protection of Human Rights Act 1993. The study was conducted for both Commissions from their inception to March, 2008. Informations contained in this book reflect only the above mentioned period and present situation means the situation of the study period. Since Non Governmental Organisations (NGOs) are grass root level workers, so attempt has been made to analyse the views of NGOs regarding the role of SHRCs in both the states.

The work is substantially based on my M.Phil. research work entitled "A study On the Role of State Human Rights Commissions in Northeast India." To give readers the actual pen picture, the study has been made by participant field work in Assam and

Manipur over a period of eighteen months in several phases.

The work will help the readers to understand the actual structural condition of AHRC & MHRC and their role in protecting human rights in respective states. The work will also help understand the perspective of NGOs in this regard.

This attempt would be successful if this work proves valuable in any way to the readers.

For further improvement comments and suggestions are welcome.

—*Author*

List of Tables

1
Introduction

The concept of human rights gained universal currency since the mid 20th century after the World War II. The devastating impact of this War compelled people and scholars to think again and again about 'humaneness'. It is this concern that prompted the United Nations Organizations (UNO) to adopt the Universal Declaration on Human Rights (UDHR) in 1948 in order to protect human being from inhuman cruelty and protect human dignity and worth. UDHR, in fact, laid the foundation for the development and practice of human rights.

These rights are fundamental prerequisites for the development of human personality and dignity. Every human being irrespective of any kind of discrimination is entitled to it. Since development of personality and dignity is dependent on these rights, these are also called 'basic rights'. Viewed from this angle, demand of human rights in every sphere of life is closely connected with the basic issue of survival.

Concept of 'human rights' is based in the idea that human beings are born free. Its basic characteristics are –

- They are universal, that is they belong to humanity irrespective of race, religion, gender, age etc.
- They are incontrovertible, that is they are absolute and innate,
- They are subjective because they are the property of individual subjects.[1]

Since the establishment of UNO several instruments such as Universal Declaration of Human Rights (UDHR), International

Covenant on Civil and Political Rights (ICCPR), International Covenant on Economic, Social and Cultural Rights (ICESCR) etc. have been adopted to ensure different rights. The signatory states have adopted the same in their countries.

The concept of 'rights' is linked with the concept of 'duties'. This implies that just as every one has rights, it is the duty of the individual to ensure that his / her enjoyment of right do not infringe the enjoyment of another person's rights. Besides, it is well known that state is the guarantor of citizens' rights; at the same time individuals too have duties towards the state.

Human rights are those rights which belong to human beings. For the enjoyment of the rights it is imperative to create social conditions wherein a person can survive and develop without hindrances. "Rights are those conditions of social life without which man cannot be as his best or give of his best, or what is needful to the adequate development and expression of his personality."[2] For Bosanquet, "A right is a claim recognized by society and enforced by the state".[3] According to E. Barker, "Rights are the external conditions necessary for the greatest possible development of the capacities of the personality".[4] According to Prof. Laski, "State is known by the rights that it maintains".[5] And rights belonging to human beings are referred as human rights.

According to A.J.M. Milne, "There can be no human community without rights. Having rights is part of what is to be member of any community. A community necessarily consists of members who have rights and obligations. Unless there are members, there cannot be community. There have to be rights if there is to be any social life. Thus, rights enable an individual with at least some of elements of a place, an identity and a role in the social milieu."[6]

According to Dr. M.R. Ansari "human rights is connected not only with the protection of individuals from the exercise of state or governmental authority in certain areas of their lives, but that it is also directed towards the creation of societal conditions by the state in which individuals may develop to their fullest potential."[7]

For David Selby, "Human Rights pertain to all persons and are possessed by everybody in the world because they are human beings, they are not earned, brought or inherited nor are they created by any contractual undertaking".[8]

Thus it can be said that human rights are certain claims supportive to the development of human dignity and personality entitled to all human beings irrespective of any kind of discrimination.

According to UDHR 'human rights' are inherent in our nature and without which we can not live as human beings.[9] It further states that "human rights and freedom allow us to fully develop and use our human qualities, our intelligence, our talents and our conscience and to satisfy our spiritual and other need."[10]

The theory and practice of 'human rights' gained momentum after the adoption of UDHR which was adopted by General Assembly on December 10, 1948. The UDHR comprises 30 articles among which first two articles are fundamental principles for all human rights. Article 3 to 21 comprises civil and political rights; article 22 to 27 comprises economic, social and cultural rights. And the last three articles are concluding ones.[11]

In 1951 after the adoption of UDHR the UNO directed the Commission on Human Rights to draft a Covenant which incorporates civil-political rights and economic-social and cultural rights. But the ideological debate between capitalist and socialist block compelled the Human Rights Commission to draw up two separate Covenants - ICCPR and ICESCR. These were adopted by the General Assembly on 16th December 1966 and came into force on 23 March 1976 and 3rd January 1976 respectively.

UDHR provides for certain standards based on moral force and it lacks legal sanctions of its own but the two Covenants being based on agreement or treaty are legally binding on the state parties.[12]

India ratified both these Covenants with some reservations on few articles on 10th April 1979. India expressed reservation on article 1(Right to Self Determination) of both the Covenants, article 9(Right to Liberty and Security), article 12 (Right to Freedom of

Movement and Residence), article13 (Rights of Alien), article19 (Right to hold opinions without interference and to freedom of expression), article 21(Right to Assemble Peacefully), article 22(Right to Freedom of Association, to form and join Trade unions) of ICCPR and article 4(Limitations may be placed on these rights only if compatible with the nature of these rights and solely for the purpose of promoting the general welfare in a democratic society), article 8(Right to form and Join Trade Unions, Right to Strike), article7(C)(equal opportunity for everyone in promotion to higher level) of ICESCR.[13]

While expressing reservation on article 1 of both the Covenants the Govt. of India declared that 'the right of self-determination applies only to people under foreign domination and not to sovereign independent States or to a section of a people or nation, which is the essence of national integrity.'[14] With reference to other articles mentioned above the Govt. of India declares that these would be so applied as to be in conformity with the provisions of article 16(4) of the Constitution of India. With respect to article 13 of the International Covenant on Civil and Political Rights, the Government reserves its right to apply its law relating to foreigners.

In spite of the fact that India expressed reservation on several articles of these Covenants the provisions of the Constitution towards providing these rights are in tune with the rights guaranteed under the two Covenants. For example articles 14 to 18 of Indian Constitution (Right to Equality) are in tune with the provisions of article 3 and 26 of ICCPR and 2 (2) and 3 of ICESCR. Article 22 of Indian Constitution deals with Protection against arrest and detention in certain cases and similar provision is contained in article 9 and 14(3) of ICCPR. Article 25 of Indian Constitution deals with freedom of conscience and free profession, practice and propagation of religion and similar provision is contained in article 18 of ICCPR. Article 27 of the ICCPR recognizes right of religious, ethnic or linguistic minorities, similar contention is also recognized in article 29 of the Indian Constitution.

Similarly article 6 (Right to Work) of ICESCR is envisaged in article 41 of the Directive Principles of State Policy (Chapter-IV). Article 7 of ICESCR recognizes the right to work in just and favourable condition and equal pay for equal work; similar provisions are there in article 42 and 43 of the Indian Constitution.

Article 41 of Indian Constitution directs the Central and State governments within the limits of its economic capacity to make effective provisions for securing the right to education and article 45 directs for free and compulsory education, similarly article 13 of ICESCR talks about right to education.

Thus while ratifying the Covenants, India reserved its certain provisions but in tune several provisions of these Covenants are similar to some of the articles of Indian Constitution itself which is prior to both the Covenants.

Indian Constitution in its Preamble upholds four objectives to run India. The Preamble recognizes social, economic and political justice for all. It also aims to recognize liberty of thought, expression, belief, faith and worship. No one can be deprived from these freedoms arbitrarily. Freedoms are recognized for the fullest development of the personality of the citizens.

Indian Constitution also recognizes equality of status and opportunity. In the Preamble fraternity is recognized as the fourth objective. The Preamble also assures 'dignity of individual'. Human rights are the part and parcel of the human dignity.

Thus it is clear that Indian Constitution from the beginning aims for the recognition and protection of human rights. And for the achievement of these aims the Constitution in Part III recognizes Fundamental Rights and in Part IV recognizes Directive Principles of state policy.

Fundamental Rights in Part-III of the Constitution are categorized into the following groups:

- Right to Equality (Articles 14 to 18)
- Right to Freedom (Articles 19 to 22)
- Right against Exploitation (Articles 23 to 24)
- Right to Freedom of Religion (Articles 25 to 28)
- Cultural and Educational Rights (Articles 29 to 30)
- Right to Constitutional Remedies (Article 32).

The above categories of rights are considered as essentials for the development of human personality and dignity.

Besides the Fundamental Rights which are mainly civil and political in nature, Indian Constitution in Part-IV (article 38 to 51) enshrined Directive Principles of State Policy which are socio-economic in nature. Although these are not enforceable by Court but these are directions to the states for securing dignified lives for its citizens.

Article 37 deals with the application of these principles. Though Directive Principles contained in Part-IV of the Constitution shall not be enforceable by any Court, but "....fundamental in the governance of the country and it shall be the duty of the state to apply these principles in making laws."[15]

Article 39(a) states that the State shall direct its policy towards securing that the citizens, men and women equally, have the right to an adequate means of livelihood. Article 41 recognizes right to work, to education and to public assistance in certain cases. Article 47 states that it is the duty of the State to raise the level of nutrition and the standard of living and to improve public health.

Thus, it can be said that fundamental rights are more meaningful in the backdrop of directive principles. In fact, without social and economic rights civil and political rights are meaningless. Directive Principles aims for creation of a society with equal socio- economic justice for all.

Besides the Constitutional provisions other measures adopted by the Government of India to protect the rights of the citizens, particularly of vulnerable sections are noteworthy. In order to protect the rights of weaker sections of society different Acts have been enacted. These are: the Dowry Prohibition Act 1961, National Commission for Minorities Act 1992, National Commission for Women Act 1990, Scheduled Castes and Schedule Tribes (prevention of atrocities) Act 1989, Immoral Traffic (prevention) Act 1956, Child Marriage Restraint Act 1924, Children Act 1960, Child Labour (Prohibition and Regulation) Act 1986, Bonded Labour (Systems Abolition) Act 1976, Right to Information Act 2005, and National Rural Employment Guarantee Act 2005, the

Protection of Women from Domestic Violence Act 2005. The enactment of the Protection of Human Rights Act 1993 is an important milestone for the protection and promotion of the rights of human beings.

The Act identifies the rights relating to life, liberty, equality, and dignity of the individual guaranteed by the Constitution or embodied in the International Covenants and enforceable by courts in India as 'human rights'[16]

This Act also provides for the constitution of National Human Rights Commission (NHRC) at the national level and State Human Rights Commissions (SHRC) at state level.

The National Human Rights Commission consists of a chairperson who has been a chief justice of the Supreme Court, a judge of Supreme Court, a chief justice of High Court, and two members to be appointed from amongst persons having knowledge of or practical experience in matters relating to human rights [Article 3 (2)]. In same way the State Human Rights Commission consists of a chairperson who has been a chief justice of a High court, a judge of a High Court or District Court and one member to be appointed from amongst persons having knowledge of or practical experience in matters relating to human rights.

As per the provision of the Act there is NHRC and few states, such as Andhra Pradesh, Assam, Chhattisgarh, Gujarat, Himachal Pradesh, Jammu and Kashmir, Kerala, Madhya Pradesh, Maharashtra, Orissa, Manipur, Punjab, Rajasthan, Tamil Nadu, Uttar Pradesh and West Bengal have constituted SHRC.

Both NHRC and SHRC are empowered to look into cases of violation of human rights; to review the safeguards provided for the protection of human rights and to recommend measures for their effective implementation.

Chapter III of the Protection of Human Rights Act 1993 deals with the powers and functions (article 12) of the NHRC.

According to article 12, NHRC shall perform all or any of the following functions, namely:[17]

a) to inquire, *suo motu* or on a petition presented to it by a victim or any person on his behalf, or on a direction or order of any Court, into complaint of

   1. violation of human rights or abetment thereof or
   2. negligence in the prevention of such violation, by a public servant;

b) intervene in any proceeding involving any allegation of violation of human rights pending before a court with the approval of such court;

c) visit, notwithstanding anything contained in any other law for the time being in force, any jail or any other institution under the control of the State Government, where persons are detained or lodged for purposes of treatment, reformation or protection, for the study of the living conditions of the inmates thereof and make recommendations thereon to the Government;

d) review the safeguards provided by or under the Constitution or any law for the time being in force for the protection of human rights and recommend measures for their effective implementation;

e) review the factors, including acts of terrorism that inhibit the enjoyment of human rights and recommend appropriate remedial measures;

f) study treaties and other international instruments on human rights and make recommendations for their effective implementation;

g) undertake and promote research in the field of human rights;

h) spread human rights literacy among various sections of society and promote awareness of the safeguards available for the protection of these rights through publications, the media, seminars and other available means;

i) encourage the efforts of non-governmental organizations and institutions working in the field of human rights;

j) such other functions as it may consider necessary for the protection of human rights.

In Chapter IV of the Act procedure for making inquiry, annual report and special reports etc have been described.

Chapter VI and VII of the Act deal with the Human Rights Court and Finance, Accounts and Audit. Article 30 of Chapter VI of the Act deals about Human Rights Courts. It says-

For the purpose of providing speedy trial of offences arising out of violation of human rights, the State Government may, with the concurrence of the Chief Justice of the High Court, by notification, specify for each district a Court of Session to be a Human Rights Court to try the said offences.

Provided that nothing in this section shall apply if

1. a Court of Session is already specified as a special court; or
2. a special court is already constituted, for such offences under any other law for the time being in force.

According to article 31 the State Government shall, by notification specify a Public Prosecutor or appoint an advocate who has been in practice as an advocate for not less than seven years, as a Special Public Prosecutor for the purpose of conducting cases in Human Rights Court.

Articles 32 and 33 of Chapter VII of the Act deal with financial sources of NHRC and SHRCs respectively. According to article 32(1)-

The Central Government shall after due appropriation made by Parliament by law in this behalf, pay to the Commission by way of grants such sums of money as the Central Government may think fit for being utilized for the purposes of this Act.

Subsection 2 of the same act says that-

The Commission may spend such sums as it thinks fit for performing the functions under this Act, and such sums shall be treated as expenditure payable out of the grants referred to in sub-section (1).

According to article 33(1)-

The State Government shall, after due appropriation made

by Legislature by law in this behalf, pay to the State Commission by way of grants such sums of money as the State Government may think fit for being utilized for the purposes of this Act.

Subsection 2 of the same act says that-

The State Commission may spend such sums as it thinks fit for performing the functions under Chapter V, and such sums shall be treated as expenditure payable out of the grants referred to in sub-section (1).

In North East India SHRCs are constituted only in Assam and Manipur. It has very significant role to play considering the socio- political condition of the region. Secessionist movements, ethnic conflicts are not uncommon for the region. Whatever may be the reason for the conflicts, these lead to the violations of the rights of the people. Moreover the policy of the Govt. of India to impose the Armed Forces Special Power Act has led to the denial of rights to the citizens of the region. Under such circumstances it is the SHRC which can play effective role for safeguarding and providing relief to the victims.

As mentioned above the Act has provided that for **the purpose of providing speedy trial of offences arising out of violation of human rights, the State Government may, with the concurrence of the Chief Justice of the High Court, by notification, specify for each district a Court of Session to be a Human Rights Court to try the said offences. But so far** no human rights court has been established in Manipur. In case of Assam we find that seven district courts had been specified as human rights courts along with the establishment of the AHRC. However, in the absence of appropriate guidelines from the Government these have become defunct at present.[18]

North East India, better identified as 'seven sisters' comprises Assam, Arunachal Pradesh, Meghalaya, Manipur, Mizoram, Nagaland, and Tripura.. Presently Sikkim is also included in that list after joining the North Eastern Council. The region is connected with mainland India only by 22km in Siliguri area of West Bengal, whereas 98% of the border of the region is with neighboring countries like Bhutan, China, Myanmar and Bangladesh.[19]

Majority of the people in the region are mongoloids and have more similarity with the peoples of Tibet, Burma and so on. As a result there is very little commonness of these people with people of rest of India. The culture of the people of this region is also varied and quite different from mainland India. The ethnic diversity is matched by linguistic diversity. The major languages of the region are Assamese, Bengali, Manipuri, Nagamese and more than 100 tribal languages/ dialects. The major tribes of this region are Chakma, Dimasa, Hojong, Tippera, Mog, Lushai, Abor, Aka, Chakma, Kachari, Aimol, Chiru etc. Most of the places lag behind in the field of infrastructure such as development of communication; basic health facilities etc. and need adequate attention. Except Guwahati in Assam no state capital of this region is connected through direct broad gauge railway connection with rest of the country even after sixty years of independence. Naturally, the backwardness of this region leads to sense of alienation from the government machineries among common people of this region.

Besides these the recent projects of the Union government for developing this region are mainly centered within the state capitals. Underdevelopment of remote districts creates centre-periphery syndrome within these states which further alienates the people from the government.

Further not much has been done to usher in industrial development. As a result the region suffers from large-scale unemployment. Unemployment problem has led to many social evils like drug abuse, extortion etc. The North Eastern Council (NEC) and Department of North Eastern Region (DONER) were established to give a fillip to the development processes but their efforts are yet to make perceptible change in the lives of the people.

The region got the attention of the rest of the country for wrong reasons. First time the Centre paid attention to the region in terms of development was in the aftermath of the Chinese aggression of 1962. The Naga and Mizo conflicts demanding independence dominated the first two decades of India's independence. Since the decade of 80s almost all parts of the region are under the effect of armed opposition groups. The major armed opposition groups in the region are United Liberation Front of Assam (ULFA), NDFB, National Liberation Front of Tripura (NLFT), Bru National Liberation Front (BNLF), National Socialist Council of Nagalim (IM & K). In Manipur, there are more than dozen groups operating for almost identical cause i.e. an independent homeland. Their activities have resulted in the destruction of public properties, kidnapping of public officials, businessmen and killing of innocent peoples. It would be no exaggeration to say that all these have led to large-scale human rights violations. In addition to this there have been ethnic clashes between the Bodos and the Santhals; between the Hmars and Dimasas in the North Cachar Hill district, among Kuki-Naga, Kuki-Paite, Meiti-Naga in Manipur; Reang-Mizo conflict in Mizoram and persecution of Khasi-Pnar tribes in Karbi-Anglong district. Displacements due to developmental projects have also added to the physical and mental anguish and sufferings of the people.

The imposition of Armed Forces Special Power Act (1958) by the Govt. of India to fight the situation has negated the rights of the people. The Act has given wide powers to the security personnel to kill, arrest without warrant etc. For example, according to article 4 of the Act –"Any commissioned officer, warrant officer, non commissioned officer or any other person of equivalent rank in the armed forces may, in a disturbed area-

(a) if he is of opinion that it is necessary so to do for the maintenance of Public order, after giving such due warning as he may consider necessary, fire upon or otherwise use force, even to the causing of death, against any person who is acting in contravention of any law or order for the time being in force in the disturbed area prohibiting the assembly of five or more persons or the carrying of weapons or of things capable of being used as weapons or of fire-arms, ammunition or explosive substances;[20]

(c) arrest, without warrant, any person who has committed a cognisable offence or against whom a reasonable suspicion exists that he has committed or is about to commit a cognisable offence and may use such force as may be necessary to effect the arrest."[21]

"No persecution, suit or other legal proceeding shall be instituted, except with the previous sanction of the Central Government, against any person in respect of anything done or purported to be done in exercise of the powers conferred by this Act (Article 6)."[22]

It indicates that any commissioned officer, warrant officer, non commissioned officer or any other person of equivalent rank in the armed forces may arrest without warrant, even shot to death and for this that army has only to say that it is necessary to do so and no legal proceedings can be taken against the army without prior permission of the central government, even the state human rights commission can not take any case against them.

Insurgency and counter-insurgency makes the region a place of gross human rights violations. In order to protect the rights of people Assam Human Rights Commission (AHRC) in Assam and Manipur Human Rights Commission (MHRC) in Manipur have been established. The importance of the role of state commissions lies in the fact that they are the government machineries to look into the human rights violation cases even done by public officials.

The problem of insurgency in Assam should be seen in historical perspective. After the annexation of Assam, the British brought Bengali people as administrators, Nepali peoples as soldiers, Marwari peoples for business purposes in Assam.[23]

Development of tea industry brought labourers from Bihar, Uttar Pradesh, Bengal.[24] After the independence influx of refugees changed the demographic structure of Assam. So, from British period influx of people for different reasons in the regions is continuing. As a result a sense of identity crisis among Assamese gentry led to anti foreigners' movement. It was a movement aimed at complete Assamization by driving out the non Assamese people from the state. Such a step had strong support of the United Liberation Front of Asom (ULFA).[25]

In Assam major armed opposition groups are United Liberation Front of Assam (ULFA) which considers itself a "revolutionary political organization" engaged in a "liberation struggle" against India for the establishment of a *sovereign, independent* Assam; National Democratic Front of Bodoland

(NDFB) which wants to create a 'sovereign Bodoland' in the areas north of the river Brahmaputra; United People's Democratic Solidarity (UPDS) seeks the secession of the Karbi-Anglong region of the North Cachar Hills district; Dima Halim Daoga (DHD) whose objective is to create a separate state of 'Dimaraji' comprising dimasa dominated areas of the N.C.Hills and Karbi Anglong districts of Assam and parts of Dimapur district in Nagaland for the Dimasa tribe; the objective of Hmar Peoples Convention – Democracy (HPC-D) is to create independent Hmar state consisting of the Hmar inhabited areas of Mizoram, Manipur and Assam. Activities of these groups cause human rights violations.

Not only the activities of extremists groups but counter insurgency operations also cause human rights violations. In Assam in the name of counter insurgency operation and protecting rights of people, Armed Forces Special Power Act 1958 has been in effect and several counter insurgency operations such as, Operation Rhino, Operation *Bajrang*, Operation *Sher-e-Dil* were conducted.

Because of the activities of the armed opposition groups and counter insurgency operations a conflict situation prevails in the state. Consequently, common sufferers are the people of the area. Murder, extrajudicial killings, rape, torture, kidnapping, sexual harassment etc have become a common phenomenon where individuals are deprived of their basic rights. Human rights situation of Assam deteriorated rapidly after the deployment of army since November 1990 (Appendix I).

South Asia Terrorism Portal (Appendix II) shows that since 1992 to 1998/2000 there had been an increase in casualties related to terrorist violence in Assam and since 2001 although the number has gone down but it continues to trouble the life of people. The 30th October 2008's serial bomb blast is the most recent example of the human rights violation in the state.

As seen from the above discussion, Assam is suffering from human rights violation since the later part of 20th century as a result of the conflict situation. In principle, the State Human Rights Commission and State Women Commission in Assam were constituted timely which is a step in the right direction of providing justice to the victims. The Assam Human Rights Commission was established in 1996.

Situated in the eastern part of India Manipur is bounded by Mizoram in the south, Assam in the west, Nagaland in the north and Myanmar in the east. It attained the status of full-fledged state on 21st January1972. The total area of the state is 22,327 sq.km. It consists of both hilly and plain regions which are inhabited by different ethnic groups. Out of the total population of 2,388,634 persons, males' number is 1,207,338 and females are 1,181,296. Handloom is the biggest industry in the state and it is the first state to introduce oak, *tsar* industry and there are 9,247 small scale industries in the state.[26]

Although there are number of small scale industries in the state but unfortunately the state till date does not show any remarkable position in the development of large scale industrialization. The common problems of the state are lack of communication, economic and social problems, feeling of alienation among people from Indian government and hindrances created by armed opposition groups in the implementation of developmental projects.

In Manipur there are as many armed opposition groups as the number of ethnic groups. However, these do not necessarily represent the ethnic identities of the people, except like KuKi, Hmar, Manipuri Pangals and so on. The major armed opposition groups in the state are People's Revolutionary Party of Kangleipak (PREPAK) which demands the expulsion of 'outsiders' from the State; Kangleipak Communist Party (KCP) which wants to restore the independence of the erstwhile Manipur kingdom from the Indian rule and to bring about an egalitarian society by uniting all ethnic-Mongoloid groups belonging to South-East of Himalayan region. People's Liberation Army (PLA) aims to liberate Manipur from India; the main objective of United National Liberation Front (UNLF) is to establish an independent socialist Manipur etc.

In 1980 in the face of turbulent activities of the armed opposition groups the state was brought under the Disturbed Area Act, 1955 following which Armed Forces Special Power Act (1958) was imposed.

As in Assam in Manipur too the imposition of this Act as well as the activities of the armed opposition group have led to widespread violations of human rights such as disappearances, extrajudicial killings, illegal detention, rape, sodomy and torture extortion. Following few incidents amply indicate the situation.

"On 2nd December, 2006, Prime Minister Dr. Manmohan Singh announced from Kangla Fort that the central government was considering amendments to the Armed Forces Special Power Act to make it 'humane.'"[27] It indicates that Union government itself agrees with the view that Armed Forces Special Power Act is inhuman but any positive action towards this direction is yet to take place.

According to South Asia Terrorism Portal (Appendix II), since 1992 to till date on an average annually more than 120 civilians are killed as a result of conflict. It indicates gross violation of human rights in the state. Apart from this up to 31st December 2005 in the two Central Jails out of 529 prisoners 31 were convicted prisoners whereas 395 were under trial prisoners.[28] There is no separate jail for women.

Under such situation the role of the State Human Rights Commission becomes very important. Manipur Human Rights Commission was established in the year 1999 and came into force in 2000 in order to protect rights of common people and to provide relief to the victims.

There is no denying of the fact that the protection and propagation of human rights is essential for safeguarding human dignity and happiness. No amount of constitutional guarantee can ensure this unless the state comes forward with suitable institutional mechanisms. The NHRC and its counterpart at the state level have been established towards achieving this goal.

In the North East India the workings of SHRCs assume significance as the large parts of the region have been existing under the shadow of insurgency and counter insurgency situations in addition to the negation of rights that the rest of citizens suffer from, such as, economic deprivation, exploitation and social injustice. Under such conditions the SHRCs can act effectively as the protector or guardian of the rights of citizens. Protection of rights involves two elements –

I. It has to see that the rights of the people are not violated;

II. wherever such violations have taken place, it has to play effective role to provide relief to the victims.

In this study it has been tried to examine the functions of these institutions and to evaluate their role from these standpoints. The book presents a theoretical and empirical analysis of the SHRC in Assam and Manipur. The provisions as laid down in the Protection of Human Rights Act, 1993 will constitute the theoretical background against which the working of SHRCs will be examined.

NOTES & REFERENCES

1. Darren J. O'Byrne, *Human Rights – An Introduction*, Pearson Education, 2004, p. 27.
2. N. Jayapalan, *Human Rights*, Atlantic Publishers and Distributors, 2000, p. 2.
3. *Ibid.*
4. *Ibid.*
5. *Ibid.*
6. Arun Roy Mohapatra, *National Human Rights Commission of India– Formation, Functioning and Future Prospects*, Radha Publications, 2001, p. 17.
7. Dr. M.R.Ansari, *Protecting Human Rights*, Maxford Books, 2006.
8. Arun Roy Mohapatra, *op. cit.*
9. Universal Declaration of Human Rights, Preamble, http://www.un.org/en/documents/udhr/
10. Universal Declaration of Human Rights, http://www.un.org/en/documents/udhr/
11. P.Kalita, S.Rajkhowa, S.C. Mohammad, *The International Bill of Human Rights*,Assam Human Rights Commission, 2001, p. 44.
12. *Ibid*, p. 51.
13. Ranju R. Dhamala, "Human Rights: Problems and Challenges", *Assam University Journal A Journal of New Ideas*, vol.1, no.1 (January 2006), p. 23.
14. *Ibid.*

15. Dr. Durga Das Basu, *Introduction to the Constitution of India*, Wadhwa and Company Law Publishers, 2004, pp. 146-147.
16. The Protection of Human Rights Act, 1993, Definitions 2(1) (d), http://nhrc.nic.in/
17. The Protection of Human Rights Act 1993, http://nhrc.nic.in/
18. Based on the information given by the functionary of AHRC.
19. Tanmoy Bhattacharjee, *Political Economy of North-East India*, Self Published, 2004, p. 247.
20. Armed Forces Special Power Act, of 1958, www.mha.nic.in/pdfs/armed_forces_special_powers_act1958.pdf
21. *Ibid.*
22. *Ibid.*
23. Chinmayee Bhattacharjee, An Interface between Insurgency and Human Rights in Northeast India, M.Phil Diss., Assam University, 2004, p. 108.
24. Tanmoy Bhattacharjee: *op.cit.*, p.268
25. Chinmayee Bhattacharjee, *op.cit.*, pp. 110-112
26. Tanmoy Bhattacharjee, *op.cit.*, pp.11-12
27. Reports of Asian Centre for Human Rights; India Human Rights Report -2007, http://www.achrweb.org/reports/india/AR07/AR2007.htm
28. Official website of NHRC, http://nhrc.nic.in/PRISON_STATS_JUN_08_FOR_NIC.xls

2

State Human Rights Commission: Formation, Structure and Functions (Assam and Manipur)

Adoption of Universal Declaration of Human Rights (UDHR) is the major landmark in the promotion and protection of human rights. The preamble of the UDHR reaffirms the fundamental necessity for the protection and promotion of human rights to save human society from barbarous acts. Basically it is the affirmation of the charter of the United Nations which states "world should reaffirm faith in fundamental human rights."[1] As discussed in the previous chapter that although UDHR provides the basis for the protection and promotion for Human Rights but ICCPR and ICESCR are the major documents or instruments which provide the legal sanction in this regard.

The concept of Human Rights as described in these instruments underlines the existence of democratic institutions promoting democratic values. It has to be remembered that the adoption of these instruments at the international level led to the promotion and protection of human rights by individual states through their own institutions as promotion of human rights and development of human rights culture are the primary responsibilities of the signatory states. It is imperative, therefore, for respective signatory member-states to adopt adequate legislation, strengthen democratic institutions and establish independent machineries both at national and local levels to monitor the implementation of the human rights legislations.

At a seminar on 'National and Local Institutions for the Promotion and Protection of Human Rights' held in Geneva from 18 to 29 September 1978 the UN set out a series of guidelines.[2] Within a broad framework of the guidelines a number of countries set up national and local institutions. In India the Protection of Human Rights Act 1993 provides the basis for the establishment of the national and state level human rights Commissions for promoting and protecting basic rights of people.

Development of Human Rights Organizations in India

In India, the concern for protecting the rights of the people existed even before the adoption of the UN Charter and UDHR as evidenced by the existence of Civil Liberties Union in 1930s, the Madras Civil Liberties Organization (1947), Civil Liberties Committee (1948). These organizations were successful in collecting information about human rights violations, providing legal aid and in creating consciousness among masses.

In the 1970s the formation of the Association for Protection of Democratic Rights (APDR) in Calcutta, and the Andhra Pradesh Civil Liberties Committee (APCLC) paved the way for the establishment of such other organizations. The APDR and APCLC focus on the exploitations in the countryside and the coercive actions of the state machineries.[3] In this connection the name of Jaya Prakash Narayan's the People's Union for Civil Liberties and Democratic Rights is worth mentioning.

The emergency period (1975-1977) during the Prime Ministership of Mrs. Indira Gandhi, led to the formation of Committee for the Protection of Democratic Rights in Bombay, Citizens for Democracy in Delhi. These organizations differ in their structures but their tasks were more or less similar like conducting awareness programmes, fact finding missions etc.

The decade of 1980s provided the essential backdrop for the adoption of the Protection of Human Rights Act 1993. The recommendations of Minorities Commission (1983) and the activities of the several civil liberties organizations to form a Human Rights Tribunal (1986)[4] had a positive effect on the policy framers to provide an institutional mechanism for the protection of the rights of the people.

Further India was criticized by organizations like Amnesty International, Asia Watch etc. in the wake of the its action against the armed opposition groups in Jammu & Kashmir, North East India as also against the Naxalites operating in different parts of the country. Besides, due to security reasons India denied the visit of these organizations to sensitive areas which helped in creating suspicion in the minds of these organizations about India's commitment towards human rights. Not only the USA and UK other countries like Sweden, Norway, France, Switzerland also expressed their concern over the violation of human rights of the country.[5] Hence, there was a need to counter these criticisms directed against India through some positive actions.

The Indian National Congress in its 1991 election manifesto promised for setting up a Human Rights Commission.

The Chief Ministers' Conference held on 14th September 1992 argued for the foundation of a Chief Ministers Committee consisting of five chief ministers including central ministers to frame guidelines for national and state level commissions. At the same time, there were several chief ministers who were against the establishment of the commissions. According to the Chief Minister of Mizoram Lalthanhawla the Constitution itself guaranteed the civil and political rights so there was no necessity for such commissions.[6] Assam Chief Minister criticized the role of some organizations and media for 'blowing custodial crimes out of proportion,' on the other hand keeping silent over other human rights violation of citizens.[7] Karnataka Chief Minister argued for separate state level human rights commission and clear demarcation of jurisdiction between state and national commission.

Viewed from the angle of the slow pace of the Indian judicial system there was a necessity of establishing a Commission as a redressal mechanism for the protection of rights. In addition to this, countries like Australia, Mexico, Algeria, Northern Ireland etc had set up their own commissions. Thus, the Govt. of India felt it necessary to show how strong India is towards its commitment in promoting and protecting human rights through the enactment of the Human Rights Protection Act 1993.

The Human Rights Commission Bill was introduced in the Lok sabha on 14th May 1992 and was referred by the Speaker to the standing committee of Parliament. The ordinance was promulgated by the President of India on 28th September 1993. Accordingly the Protection of Human rights Act 1993 came into force.

State Human Rights Commission

The Protection of Human Rights Act 1993 provides provisions for the establishment of SHRCs in states. Article 21 deals with the constitution of SHRCs.

According to article 21(1) - A State Government may constitute a body to be known as the... (Name of the State) Human Rights Commission to exercise the powers conferred upon, and to perform the functions assigned to, a State Commission under this chapter.

According to article 21(2) the State Commission shall, with effect from such date as the State Government may by notification specify, consists of-

1. a Chairperson who has been a Chief Justice of a High Court;
2. one Member who is, or has been, a Judge of a High Court or District Judge in the State with a minimum of seven years experience as District Judge.
3. one Member to be appointed from amongst persons having knowledge of, or practical experience in, matters relating to human rights.

It is important to mention here that when the Act came into force in 1993, there was the provision that the Commission to be constituted with five Members. But subsequently in 2006 an amendment was passed by the Indian Parliament which underlies that Commission has to be constituted with three Members. So, when we look at the first Commission of both AHRC and MHRC we will find five Members including the Chairperson but when we look at the present set up we may find three Members as the amendment of the act specify.

Assam Human Rights Commission

As we have seen in the introductory chapter the human rights situation in Assam is a matter of great concern. In Assam the conflict situation centering on the demand for independent homeland raised by groups like ULFA, NDFB and others has caused a sense of insecurity and brought sufferings for the people. Both government security forces and armed opposition groups are responsible for human rights violations. In addition to this the poor condition in which people are forced to live negates the basic rights of the people. Poor road condition, poor sanitation system, unhygienic conditions of hospitals, jails etc., present a negative picture of the state delivery system. Hence, the establishment of state human rights commission was considered necessary.

In exercise of the powers conferred under section 21(1) of the Protection of Human Rights Act 1993 the Governor of Assam[8] in 1996 for the first time constituted a body known as the Assam Human Rights Commission to exercise the powers conferred upon, and to perform the functions assigned to State Commission under Chapter – V of the Act.

The Governor of Assam[9] constituted the Assam State Human Rights Commission with the following persons:

1. Hon'ble Mr. Justice Surendra Nath Bhargava (Retired Chief Justice of Gauhati High Court): Chairperson
2. Hon'ble Mr. Justice T.C.Das (Retired Judge of Gauhati High Court): Member
3. Mr. Paramananda Kalita (Former District Judge): Member
4. Mr. Sheikh Chand Mohammad (Former Speaker, Assam Legislative Assembly) Member
5. Mr. Robindra Nath Barooah (Former Editor, The *Assam Tribune*): Member

As discussed earlier, in 1996 according to original Act there was provision for five members Commission including the Chairperson which was subsequently amended in 2006 and was reduced to three members including the Chairperson. The inauguration programme of the office of the Assam Human Rights

Assam Human Rights Commission, Guwahati

Commission (AHRC) was held on 16th November, 1996 in the STATFED building, Guwahati, Assam which was attended among others by the Chairperson of National Human Rights Commission Hon'ble Mr. Justice R.N.Misra, Chief Minister and some other cabinet members of Assam, Chief Secretary to the Government of Assam, Chairperson of the Assam State Commission for Women, representatives of several NGOs and others.

The Chairperson and the members assumed office on the dates mentioned below:[10]

1. Hon'ble Mr. Justice Surendra Nath Bhargava as Chairperson on March 26, 1996.
2. Hon'ble Mr. Justice T.C.Das as Member on April 4, 1996.
3. Mr. Paramananda Kalita as Member on May 1, 1996.
4. Mr. Sheikh Chand Mohammad as Member on March 29, 1996.

The fifth member Mr. Rabindra Nath Barooah could not join the Commission as he attained the age of 70 years before the date of order of the constitution of the state Commission was issued.

Chart 2.1
Structure of Assam Human Rights Commission

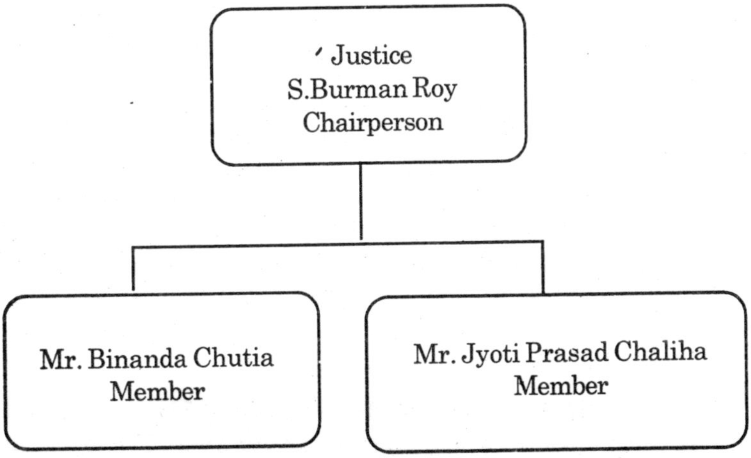

Source: Office of the Assam Human Rights Commission

Sri Ahindra Kr. Choudhury, IAS (Retd.) joined as the secretary of the Assam Human Rights Commission. Sri Shankar Baruah, IPS, Inspector General of Police (Training and Armed Police) Assam joined on 3/2/97 as Director of Investigation of the SHRC in addition to his regular duties as IGP (T and P) Assam.

At present, the Assam Human Rights Commission comprise the Chairperson, who had been a Chief Justice of a High Court and a member who had been a Judge of District Court and a member who had been a principal of a Govt. Degree College of Assam appointed by a duly constituted committee for this purpose (Chart No. 2.1).

Manipur Human Rights Commission

Like Assam, as discussed in chapter 1, the human rights situation of Manipur is also a serious matter of concern. There are innumerable numbers of cases of human rights violations and the violators go unpunished. In order to protect and ensure the rights of the people several NGOs in the field of Human Rights organized seminars, workshops to find a solution to the problem. They were univocal in their demand for the establishment of governmental machinery with the exclusive responsibility of safeguarding and furthering the rights of the people. The adoption of the Protection of Human Rights Act 1993 thus provided impetus to the demand of establishment of state human rights commission.

Answering to a long felt aspiration of the people of Manipur the Govt. of Manipur constituted the Manipur Human Rights Commission by notification issued on 27th June 1998. The Governor Shri Oudh Narayan Shrivastava on the same day issued the warrant of appointment of Justice Surendra Nath Bhargava as the Chairperson of the Manipur Human Rights Commission. The Chairperson assumed office on 27th June 1998 in a formal function addressed by Chief Minister, some cabinet members, Chief Secretary and other dignitaries of Manipur.

On 10th December 1998 the Governor of Manipur issued appointments of other members of the Commission. The Manipur

Human Rights Commission (MHRC) started functioning with all members assuming office on the 50th anniversary of the Universal Declaration of Human Rights (10/12/98), which is also the International Human Rights Day, in a function addressed by Prof. Gangmumei Kamei, Minister of Law, state of Manipur and Prof. B.K. Roy Burman, a social anthropologist and Nehru Fellow.

The first Manipur Human Rights Commission consisted of the following members:[11]

1. Hon'ble Mr. Justice Surendra Nath Bhargava (Retired Chief Justice of Gauhati High Court): Chairperson
2. Mr. Justice Y. Ibotombi Singh (Retired Judge of Gauhati High Court): Member
3. Mr. L. Rabindra Singh (Retired District Judge of Manipur): Member
4. Mr. Yambem Laba (Journalist): Member
5. Mr. Kh. Chonjohn Singh (Advocate): Member.

Although MHRC was formed with very high hopes as to safeguard against the human rights abuses, it is sad to note that on 9th December 1998 i.e. just a day before the MHRC started functioning Shri Yambem Laba, member of the MHRC was picked up by the army in spite of his having the warrant of appointment issued by the Governor of Manipur.[12]

The full Commission met for the first time on the 22nd January 1999 and made its regulations to regulate its own procedure in exercise of the powers conferred by subsection (2) of section 10 read with section 29 of the Human Rights Protection Act.[13]

In case of Manipur Human Rights Commission the Chairperson had been a Chief Justice of a High Court, two Members were Judges of District Courts, one Member is a retired Lt. Col. As discussed earlier that although the Protection of Human Rights Act 1993 laid down provision for the appointment of five members including the Chairperson in the Commission but the subsequent amendment of 2006 reduced it to three members. The present

Chart 2.2

Structure of Manipur Human Rights Commission

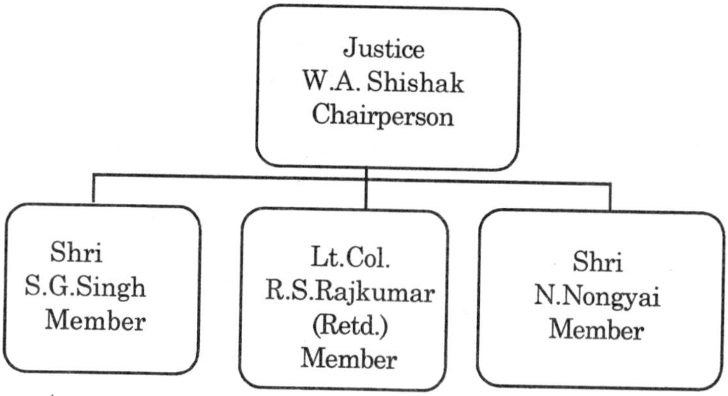

Source: Office of the Manipur Human Rights Commission

Manipur Human Rights Commission, Imphal

MHRC is constituted with four members as they were appointed in 2005 (Chart No. 2.2) i.e., prior to the amendment of the Protection of Human Rights Act 1993 in the year 2006.

Appointing Authority

According to Article 22 (1), of the said Act, the Chairperson and members of the State Commission are appointed by the Governor by warrant under his hand and seal as recommended by a appointing committee comprising the Chief Minster of the concerned state as Chairperson, Speaker of the Legislative Assembly, Minister of Home Department of the state, Opposition Leader of the Legislative Assembly as members. Although sitting Judge of a High Court or a sitting District Judge can be appointed only after consultation with the Chief Justice of the High Court of the concerned state.

Removal

Article 23, subsection 1 and 1(A) of the Act lays down principles for the removal of the Commission members. A Chairperson or a member may resign by writing a notice under his hand to Governor of the state. The Chairperson or any member of the State Commission can be removed by the President's order on the ground of proved misbehavior or incapacity according to the recommendation by Supreme Court following the inquiry about the matter as referred to it.

Till date there is no case of removal either in Assam Human Rights Commission or in Manipur Human Rights Commission.

Term

According to Article 24 (1) and (2) a person appointed as Chairperson or member of the state Commission shall hold office for a term of five years from the date on which he enters upon his office or until the age of 70 years, whichever is earlier. On ceasing to hold office, a Chairperson or a member shall be ineligible for further employment under the state or central government.

Vacancy of the Office of the Chairperson

In the event of the occurrence of any vacancy in the office of the Chairperson by reason of his death, resignation or otherwise the Governor of the state may by notification, authorize one of the members to act as the Chairperson until the appointment of a new Chairperson to fill such vacancy (Article 25(1) of the Protection of Human Rights Act, 1993).

Article 25(2) of the same act lays down that when the Chairperson is unable to discharge his functions owing to absence on leave, or otherwise, such one of the members as the Governor may, by notification, authorize in this behalf, shall discharge the functions of the Chairperson until the date on which the Chairperson resumes his duties.

Headquarter of the Commission

Article 21 (4) of the Act specifies that the headquarters of the State Commission shall be at such place as the state government may, by notification specify.

In Assam the headquarter of Assam Human Rights Commission is located in Guwahati, the state capital as specified by state government and in Manipur it is located in Imphal, the capital of Manipur.

Officers and other staff of the State Commission

Article 27(1) of the Act provides that the state government shall make available to the Commission an officer not below the rank of a secretary to the state government who shall be the secretary of the State Commission and such police and investigation staff under an officer not below the rank of an Inspector General of Police and such other officers and staffs as necessary for the efficient performance of the functions of the state commission. The state commission also may appoint such other administrative, technical and scientific staffs considered necessary, in accordance with the rules made by the state government.

Secretary

As a Chief Executive Officer of the Commission, all the orders and decisions taken by the Commission are authenticated by the secretary. All the staff of the Commission comes under the overall administrative control of the secretary who is directly responsible to the Commission. Being the chief coordinator of the Commission the secretary also keeps contact with various departments.

In Assam Human Rights Commission the Chef Executive Officer is an I.A.S., and equivalent to the rank of secretary to the Government of Assam as specified in the Act. He is not a full time secretary but hold this office in addition to his regular duties under Government of Assam.

In case of Manipur Human Rights Commission the executive head of the Commission is an officer equivalent to the rank of deputy secretary to the government of Manipur, i.e. below the rank of secretary to the state government as specified in the act. The deputy secretary of Manipur Human Rights Commission is the deputy secretary of department of law, government of Manipur and the works as deputy secretary of Manipur Human Rights Commission is his additional duty with regular duties in law department.

Investigation

Assam Human Rights Commission

Assam Human Rights Commission has investigation setup. The head of the team i.e. the Director of the investigation unit is an Inspector General of Police as laid down in the Act. In this investigation team there are two Superintendents of Police on contract basis under the director, two inspectors, and four constables. It is notable to mention that all the officials of this investigation branch are not the staff of AHRC, basically these officials are permanent employees of police department, Govt. of Assam and the duty of AHRC is their additional duty. So, in this respect we can say that the AHRC does not have its own investigation setup.

Manipur Human Rights Commission

Presently, the Manipur Human Rights Commission does not have any investigation team of its own. Only in the initial years of its establishment one Inspector General of Police was deputed to Manipur Human Rights Commission. At that time he was originally a staff of police department, Govt. of Manipur and MHRC was his additional charge but it was also withdrawn in 2000.

For the purpose of investigation Manipur Human Rights Commission, in cases of human rights violations, sends request letters to concerned officer in charge of the particular police station or superintendent of police of that district or any other concerned police officer of the police department. And Manipur Human Rights Commission has to rely on reports of police in human rights violation cases.

Administration

Assam Human Rights Commission

The division of work is not clear. Although responsibilities of work are distributed among different staff but as there is lack of staff naturally everyone is helping each other in disbursing the work. There is one deputy secretary, one superintendent, one upper division assistant, three lower division assistants, one computer and one typing assistants and six peons. From deputy secretary to peons all the members of the staff are the permanent staff of the Commission (Chart No. 2.3).

Individual persons are there for legal, accounts, administrative and establishment etc. works.

But the staffs work coordinately with each other as divisions of work are not separated due to the lack of staff.

Manipur Human Rights Commission

The division of work in Manipur Human Rights Commission (MHRC) is also not clear. Although there are some staff like one head clerk, two private secretaries, one senior accountant, four lower division clerks , four drivers, and two peons. But till date

Chart 2.3: Structure of Office of Assam Human Rights

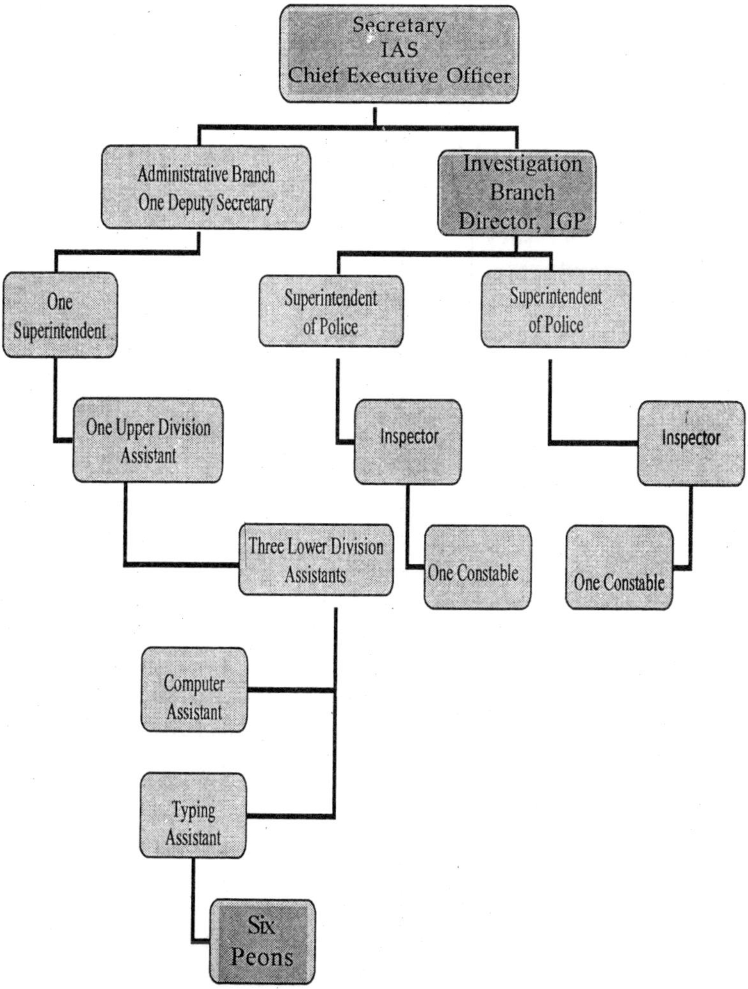

Source: Office of the Assam Human Rights Commission

Chart 2.4

Structure of the Manipur Human Rights Commission

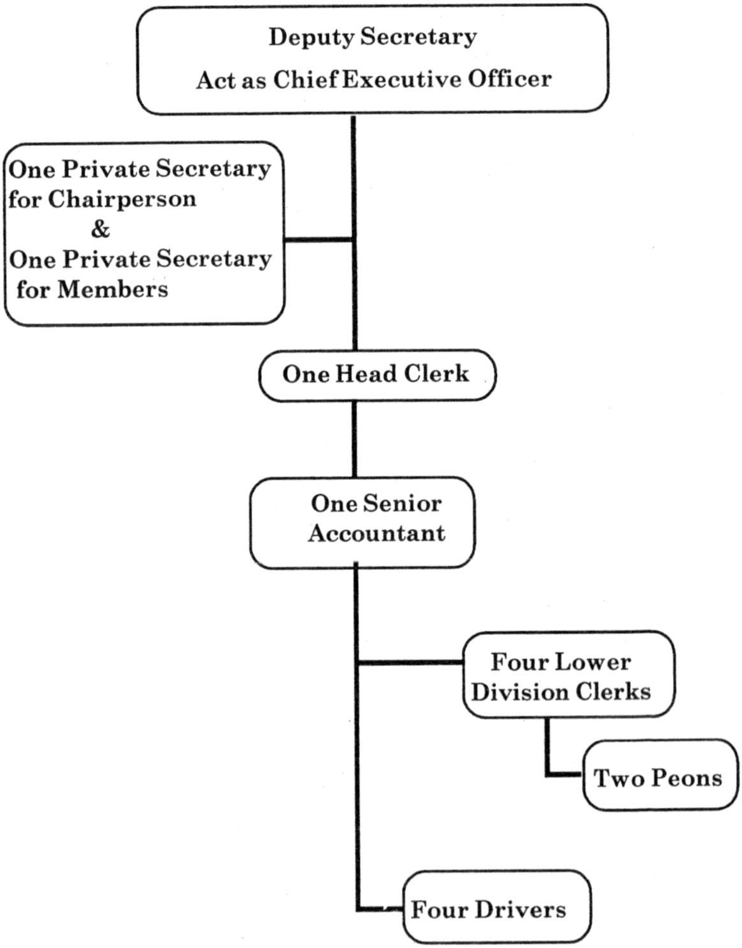

Source: Office of the Manipur Human Rights Commission

there is not a single permanent staff in the Commission. Every year a new batch of staff are provided by the state government to the Commission. (Chart No. 2.4).

Since the work divisions are not clear, all the members and the staffs coordinate with each other for the disbursement of their work. They together disburse the legal, administrative, establishment, information and public relation related works.

In case of both the SHRCs the office makes a formal registration of the case once it receives complaints. It also informs the petitioner and the accused about the action taken or likely to be taken on the case.

After registration the case is referred to decision making body of the Commission. All these works can be referred as legal works. The decision making body may

1. Dismiss the complaint -
   a) when the matter is pending before a state constituted commission or any other commission.
   b) when the matter is registered at the Commission after the expiry of one year from the date on which the act is committed.
2. dispose the case with directions to the authorities.
3. where the Commission so deems, it may call for investigations from concerned authorities and on receiving enquiry report it may pass the final order. While the AHRC has its own investigation team but the MHRC does not have any investigation team of its own, it has to rely on the enquiry reports from police or other concerned authorities.

The office of the Commission provide the administrative support to the Commission, such as, organizing the meetings of full Commission , sittings of the Commission, issuing notices for meetings, protocol arrangements etc. In AHRC day to day affairs and general works are looked after primarily by the deputy secretary. The secretary comes to the office as per necessity as he is still in his substantive position as secretary to the Govt. of

Assam. In MHRC daily affairs and general works are done under the direction of a head clerk.

Library

Both the AHRC and MHRC maintain library in its premises. These contain mainly books on law and human rights. Comparatively, the library of MHRC is smaller than the library of AHRC and does not remain open all the time.

Assam Human Rights Commission

There are two rooms one for the use of the Chairperson and another is library cum computer room. There are number of cubicles for one member, secretary, deputy secretary, accountant, personal assistant to chairperson, and other staff members. Basic facilities like computers (06 in number) with internet connectivity, vehicle, telephone, fax machine and photocopying machine are there.

Manipur Human Rights Commission

There are few differences between the AHRC and MHRC so far as infrastructural facilities are concerned. The office of the MHRC is housed in a nine room building. Out of these, four are designated for the use of the Chairperson and three members; one for private secretaries, one for deputy secretary, one office room, one court room for Commission, and one is store cum library room. Basic facilities like computers (02) with internet connectivity, vehicle (04), telephone, fax machine and photocopying machine are there.

Status of State Commissions

In spite of the independent, impartial, accessible judiciary the existence of National Human Rights Commission and State Commissions indicate their importance in the protection and enhancement of human rights. The status of the SHRCs is not only derived from statute but also from various other sources like the appointment of a retired Chief Justice of a High Court as its chairperson which generally increases the value of the

Commission. The status of the State Commission also lies in its autonomy. The Commission derives its autonomy from the method of appointment of its members, their fixity of tenure and statutory guarantee thereto, the status they have been accorded and the manner in which the staff including investigation agency are responsible to the Commission.

Functions of the State Commissions

As per the article 12 and 29(c), the State Commission performs all or any of the following functions. These are:

a) inquire, *suo motu* or on a petition presented to it by a victim or any person on his behalf or on a direction or order of any court , into complaints of-

   i) violation of human rights or abetment thereof; or

   ii) negligence in the prevention of such violation, by a public servant ;

b) intervene in any proceeding involving any allegation of violation of human rights pending before a court with the approval of such court;

c) visit, notwithstanding anything contained in any other law for the time being in force , any jail or other institution under the control of the state government, where persons are detained or lodged for purposes of treatment , reformation or protection, for the study of the living conditions of the inmates thereof and make recommendations thereon to the Government ;

d) review the safeguards provided by or under the constitution or any law for the time being in force for the protection of human rights and recommend measures for their effective implementation;

e) review the factors, including acts of terrorism that inhibit the enjoyment of human rights and recommend appropriate remedial;

f) undertake and promote research in the field of human rights;

g) spread human rights literacy among various sections of society and promote awareness of the safeguards available for the protection of these rights through publications, the media, seminars and other available means;

h) encourage the efforts of non- governmental originations and institutions working in the field of human rights; and

i) such other functions as it may consider necessary for the protection of human rights.

Powers of State Commissions

For the purpose of protecting human rights the Commission has wide-ranging powers. While inquiring into complaints the Commission can exercise all the powers of a civil court trying a suit under the Code of Civil Procedure, 1908, and in particular in respect of the following matters-

a) summoning and enforcing the attendance of witnesses and examining them on oath;

b) discovery and production of any document;

c) receiving evidence on affidavits;

d) requisitioning any public record or copy thereof from any court or office;

e) issuing Commissions for the examination of witnesses or documents; and

f) any other matter which may be prescribed.

Further the Commission has also power to require any person subject to any privilege, may enter in any building or place for searching etc. when it (the commission) has reason to believe that such inquiry may be useful.

Any proceeding before the Commission shall be deemed be a judicial proceeding within the meaning of Section 193 and 228 and for the purposes of Section 196 of the Indian Penal Code. Further the Commission shall be deemed to be a civil court for the all purposes of Section 195 and Chapter XXVI of the Code of Criminal Procedure, 1973.[14]

The Commission also has the power, for the purpose of conducting any investigation pertaining to the inquiry, utilize the services of any officer or investigation agency of the central government or the state government according to case.[15]

The officer or agency whose services are utilized shall investigate into any matter pertaining to the inquiry and submit a report thereon to the commission within the specified period by the commission.[16]

The Commission shall satisfy itself about the correctness of the facts stated and if any conclusion is arrived at in the submitted report to it, the commission may even make inquiry (including the examination of the person or persons who conducted or assisted in the investigation) as it thinks fit.[17]

Procedure and Regulations of the State Commissions

For the purpose of discharging the functions the state commissions followed certain procedures and regulations.

a) *Inquiry into Complaints*[18]

The Commission while inquiring into the complaints of violations of human rights may call for information or report from the state government or any other authority or organization subordinate thereto within such time as may be specified by it. And if the information or report is not received within the time stipulated by the Commission, it may proceed to inquire into the complaint on its own. On the other hand, if, on receipt of information or report, the Commission is satisfied that no further inquiry is required or that the required action has been initiated or taken by the concerned Government or authority, it may not proceed with the complaint and inform the complainant accordingly.

b) *Steps during and after Inquiry*[19]

The Commission may take any of the following steps during or upon the completion of an inquiry -

a) where the inquiry discloses the commission of violation of human rights or negligence in the prevention of violation of human rights by a public servant , it may recommend to the concerned government or authority-

I. to take payment of compensation or damages to the complainant or to the victim or the members of his family as the commission may consider necessary;

II. to initiate proceedings for prosecution or such other suitable action as the Commission may deem fit against the concerned person or persons;

III. to take such further action as it may think fit;

b) approach the Supreme Court or the High Court concerned for such directions, orders or writs as that Court may deem necessary;

c) recommend to the concerned government or authority at any stage of the inquiry for the grant of such immediate interim relief to the victim or the members of his family as the Commission may consider necessary;

d) subject to the provisions of clause (e) , of article 18 of the Protection of Human Rights Act, 1993, provide a copy of the inquiry report to the petitioner or his representative;

e) send a copy of its inquiry report together with its recommendations to the concerned government or authority and the concerned government or authority shall , within a period of one month, or such further time as the Commission may allow , forward its comments on the report , including the action taken or proposed to be taken thereon, to the Commission;

f) publish inquiry report together with the comments of the concerned government or authority, if any, and the action taken or proposed to be taken by the concerned government or authority on the recommendations of the Commission.

The human rights condition of both Assam and Manipur necessitates the establishment of AHRC and MHRC and accordingly these Commissions were established as per the provisions of the Protection of Human Rights Act 1993. As these Commissions are established to protect and promote human rights and investigate the cases of human rights violations, the structure itself designed in such a way as to ensure the independence of these Commissions. The prestigious post of Chairperson is held by retired Chief Justice of a High Court which automatically increases the dignity of the position of Chairperson of SHRC. For this reason inspite of being a recomendary body only in cases of human rights violations SHRC's recommendations are complied by the government of both the states.

In terms of infrastructure including the administrative staff position both the Commissions are far behind but so far the composition of the Commissions are concerned both of them are full fledged. The only disheartening point is that the Commissions do not have their own independent investigation teams, which, to some extent, hampers the independence and impartiality of the Commissions.

NOTES & REFERENCES

1. Charter of the United Nations, http://www.un.org/en/documents/charter/preamble.shtml
2. Fact sheet No. 19, National Institutions for the Promotion and Protection of Human Rights, www.ohchr.org/Documents/Publications/FactSheet19en.pdf.
3. Arun Ray Mohapatra, *op.cit.*, p. 50.
4. *Ibid.*
5. *Ibid.*
6. *Ibid.*
7. *Ibid.*
8. Vide order No.PLA/362/94/51 dated 19/3/96, News Letter, Assam Human Rights Commission, Vol.1, No.1 (January 1997).
9. Order No.PLA/362/94/51 (A), Ibid.
10. Assam Human Rights Commission. *Annual Report 1996-97*, p. 3.
11. *Newsletter*, Manipur Human Rights Commission, Vol.1, No.1 (10th May 1999)

12. *Ibid.*
13. *Ibid.*
14. Assam Human Rights Commission, *Annual Report 1996-97*, p. 6.
15. *Ibid*, p. 7.
16. *Ibid*
17. *Ibid*, p. 8.
18. The Protection of Human Rights Act, 1993, Article 17 www.nhrc.nic.in
19. The Protection of Human Rights Act, 1993, Article 18, *op.cit.*

3

Role of the State Human Rights Commission: Assam and Manipur

We have seen in the preceding chapters that for the protection of human rights there is the National Human Rights Commission at the national level to enquire into the cases of human rights violations, and the State Human Rights Commissions (SHRC) in different states to discharge the same functions at the state level. Human rights situations in the Northeast India as discussed in first chapter shows that SHRCs have an important role to play in developing human rights culture in the region. The structure and functions of SHRCs are provided in the Protection of Human Rights Act 1993. One of the main functions of these organizations is to protect and promote the human rights. For this purpose it is essential that they should have access to facts which are based on proper investigations. It implies that investigation and fact finding constitute important functions of these bodies. For a proper and effective working it is essential that these bodies have adequate finance. Objective recommendations of the commission lead to its growth, survival and its acceptability to public though it does not have the power to implement its recommendations. In short, investigation, fact finding, adequate finance and objective recommendation constitute the backbone of these institutions.

In this chapter we propose to examine the role of SHRCs in Assam and Manipur with reference to their functions, powers and working.

In general SHRC try to enquire into complains, spread human rights literacy in order to promote awareness and also protect rights of the people. These can also be treated as their objectives.

Working of the SHRC

Assam Human Rights Commission (AHRC)

The most important function of the AHRC is to inquire *suo motu* or on a petition presented to it by a victim or any person on behalf of the victim regarding the complaints of human rights violations or of negligence in the prevention of such violation by a public servant. The Commission may also intervene in any proceeding involving any allegation of violation of human rights pending before the court, with the approval of such court. Further, it can visit any jail or any other institution under intimation to and control of the State Government where persons are detained or lodged for purposes of treatment, reformation or protection in order to study the living conditions of the inmates and to make

Table 3.1 Statement of Cases between 1996[1] and 31st March 2007

i)	Total number of cases registered (Including 460 cases registered against police personnel)	:	6189
ii)	Total number of cases disposed of	:	4684
iii)	No. of cases under process	:	1505
iv)	No. of cases registered against police	:	668
v)	No. of cases registered against police disposed of	:	460
vi)	No. of cases registered against police under process	:	208
vii)	No. of custodial death cases registered	:	360
viii)	Total number of recommendations (Departmental Action & Interim Compensations)	:	73
ix)	Total number of recommendations complied with	:	45
x)	Compliance report yet to be received	:	26

Source: Office of the Assam Human Rights Commission

recommendations; review the safeguards (given by or under the constitution) meant for the protection of human rights and recommend measures for their effective implementation; review the factors (including act of terrorism) that inhibit the enjoyment of human rights and recommend appropriate remedial measures; undertake and promote research in the filed of human rights; spread human rights literacy and promote awareness regarding the means available for the protection; encourage the efforts of non-governmental organizations and institutions working in the field of human rights; and other functions as it may consider necessary for the promotion of human rights.

From the records available in the office of the Assam Human Rights Commission it is seen that the Commission has actively registered many cases of human rights violations. The cases registered with the AHRC since its inception till December 2007 is presented in Table 3.1.

Table 3.2
Year-wise Position of Cases till 31st March 2007

Year	*No. of Cases Registered*	*No. of Cases Disposed*
1996-97	471	445
1997-98	1359	1276
1998-99	892	670
1999-2000	466	425
2000-2001	278	228
2001-2002	380	265
2002-2003	605	405
2003-2004	470	333
2004-2005	407	221
2005-2006	449	203
2006-2007	412	213

Source: Office of the Assam Human Rights Commission

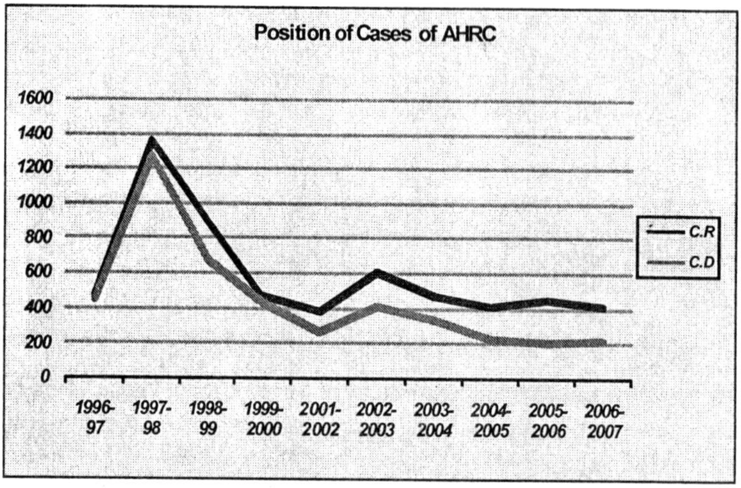

C.R. – Cases Registered C.D. - Cases Disposed

From the above chart it is evident that maximum number of cases were registered and disposed in the beginning. However, after the initial enthusiasm the numbers of cases registered and disposed started decreasing. Another important thing is that in the initial years the gap between cases registered and disposed off is very low. As for example, in 1996-97 and 1997-98 out of the total cases registered 94.5% cases and 93.89% cases were disposed off respectively. After 1998 we see the gap between the two is increasing. In 2005-06 and 2006-2007 the percentage of cases disposed off stood at 45.21% and 51.7% respectively. Such a situation casts negative image so far as the working of the AHRC is concerned. Since its establishment AHRC has received 6189 complaints among which 4684 cases have been disposed. These cases covered several aspects of violation of human rights such as, cases of disappearance, rape, custodial deaths, irregularity in providing basic services etc.

Selective study of the cases undertaken by the AHRC

In order to understand the nature of the cases registered and disposed by the AHRC a few cases are presented below.

Following case studies will give us some ideas about how the Commission is handling the cases since its inception. The sources of these cases are judgment orders and documents collected from Assam Human Rights Commission.

Case No. 1

Complain against Guwahati Municipal Corporation for insufficient supply of water AHRC Case No. 3909 of 2002

'A' and others of Rajgarh 1st Bye Lane, Guwahati, filed a complaint petition in the year 2001 before the Commission alleging insufficient supply of water by the Guwahati Municipal Corporation. It was further alleged that the amount of frequency of water supply had been deteriorated to such a level that sustaining life had become impossible. The complainant also alleged that some of the persons of the locality used to draw Municipal Corporation water by using pump directly from the line. The Commission after considering the overall aspect of the matter passed an order dated 5.10.2001 directing the Municipal Corporation to improve the water supply position to the concerned locality and also to check drawing Municipal water directly from the pipeline with the help of electrically operated pump by some consumer.

The complainant again filed a complaint petition dated 14.5.2002 before the Commission drawing the attention to the miserable state of water supply in their locality for the last 3(three) years from the date of complaint. In the petition she had referred to the earlier complaint in AHRC Case No.3504/2001. It was stated in the petition that since November 2001 till the middle of March 2002 there was temporary improvement in the water supply in the locality but then the situation deteriorated miserably and presently they were facing a state where sustaining life had become impossible as there was no other source like ground water anywhere in the area.

Acting upon the said complaint, the Commission issued notice to the Commissioner Guwahati Municipal Corporation calling for his report on the matter. Accordingly, the Commissioner, Guwahati Municipal Corporation, Guwahati submitted a report dated

10.4.2003. It was stated in the report that the water supply to the Rajgarh Road Bye-lane No.1 was made from the Water Reservoir situated at Sarania Hills. The water to the Reservoir was supplied from the treatment plant at Panbazar. It also stated that the Guwahati Municipal Corporation had taken all efforts to provide regular water supply to the rate payers of the area and the previous defects in the distribution system had been rectified. It was also submitted that the water supply system depended upon regular electricity supply from the Assam State Electricity Board (ASEB). For the last few months the power supply to the treatment plant had been found irregular due to frequent load shedding and low voltage of power which ultimately led to short supply of water to the Reservoir at Sarania Hills. Further, there was also occasional breakdown of machinery and distribution network leading to disruption of water supply to the area.

The Commission in the judgment order opined that a civic body like a Municipal Board/Corporation is under obligation to provide the basic necessity like water supply to the rate payers. The problem of insufficient supply of water is not a problem peculiar to the area of Rajgarh Bye-lane No.1 alone. It appeared to the Commission that the problem of scarcity of water supply faced by the rate payers of the area is a continuing one and the complainant and other residents of the locality had been fighting for redressal of their grievance regarding scanty water supply since a longtime. As already stated above that the complainant on earlier occasion also approached the Commission in this regard and appropriate orders were passed by the Commission directing the Municipal Authority to take necessary steps to maintain regular supply of water to the area and immediately following the order, the acute problem of insufficient water supply was somewhat eased but as alleged by the complainant, the problem continued to subsist. During the pendency of this proceeding, the complainant informed the Commission vide her letter dated 26.2.2003 that there had been remarkable improvement in the Municipal Water supply to the Rajgarh ByeLane No.1 since October 2002, but the position thereafter, started to deteriorate again.

In view of the above position and considering all aspects of the matter the Commission directed the Municipal Corporation to take steps to improve the water supply position to the concerned locality and also to take appropriate steps to check drawing of Municipal water directly from the pipeline with the help of electrically operated pumps by some consumers without any authority. The Commission in its judgment order hoped and trusted that the Guwahati Municipal Corporation shall take effective steps for ensuring adequate supply of water to the locality and thereby discharge its obligations towards the Municipal rate payers. With the above observation, the Commission closed this case.

Case No. 2

Case of negligence against a Doctor by the Barak Human Rights Protection Committee (AHRC Case No. 4436 of 2003)

The Barak Human Rights Protection Committee, Silchar, Cachar, filed a complaint petition on the basis of a news item which appeared in a local Bengali daily newspaper dated 5th March, 2003. According to the said newspaper, due to the negligence of Dr. 'A', the then Medical & Health Officer of Latu Primary Health Centre, one 'B', a student of Class-V, lost the fingers of his left hand. Dr. 'A' had stated that he did not treat the patient.

The Commission had received a report[2] from the Joint Director of Health Services, Karimganj. The Joint Director in his report had enclosed the statement of Dr. 'A', the then Medical & Health Officer of Latu Primary Health Centre. The Joint Director had also asked the Superintendent of Karimganj Civil Hospital to submit a detailed report on the matter.

In view of the objection filed by the complainant the Commission got the matter enquired by the Superintendent of Police (Investigation) of the Commission who in his report had stated that Dr. 'A' wrongly treated the patient resulting handicap for life and there was violation of human rights. The Commission issued show cause notice to Dr. 'A' who filed his reply. The Commission also summoned him and recorded his statement on 19.08.2006.

'B', s/o 'C', had fall from the roof of a building on 28th Nov, 2002 resulting in facture on his left hand. According to the complainant, he was taken to the Latu Mini PHC for treatment and Dr. 'A' put bandage on his left hand very tightly as a result of which there was swelling and infection.

From the report of Dr. 'D' of Karimganj Civil Hospital the Commission found that the injured boy was admitted on 28.12.2002 after one month of the injury. In the Civil Hospital he was given treatment and he was advised surgery of the left hand but the attendant declined to do so, on account of his poverty. The injured boy was again taken to the Civil Hospital on 1.1.2003 and he was given treatment and ultimately on 21.1.2003 his fingers were amputed. From the said report the Commission also found that after the injury he was treated by a village Doctor.

From the statement of Dr. 'A' the Commission found that on 28th November, 2002 after the closure of the dispensary the Doctor was about to go to Karimganj to get his wife treated who was in advance stage of pregnancy. The father of 'B' requested Dr. 'A' to give some treatment but Dr. 'A' informed that he was about to leave for Karimganj. Dr. 'A' offered both the father and the injured son to take them to Karimganj in his vehicle but they refused. Subsequently, he saw the boy near the Mini PHE and on being asked the injured boy informed him that he was getting treatment from a village *Kabiraj* who had given some oil for massage. According to Dr. 'A', due to not getting proper treatment the boy lost the fingers of his left hand. The father of the boy gave a written petition to the Joint Director of Health Services, Karimganj stating that Dr. 'A' was not responsible but due to his poverty he could not get his boy treated as per advice of Dr. 'A'. About 100 persons of the village submitted a petition before the Commission giving full facts stating that the allegations against Dr. 'A' were baseless.

From the facts the Commission found that after one month of getting injury the boy was not taken to the Civil Hospital and it proved the fact that the boy was treated by a village *Kabiraj* who was not a qualified Doctor and as a result the boy suffered and ultimately his finger was amputed.

The Commission in their judgment order stated that the Commission could not find any fault with Dr. 'A' and, accordingly dismissed the show cause notice against Dr. 'A'. The Commission also stated that it was evident that due to negligence of the father of the injured boy the unfortunate thing had happened.

Case No. 3

Case of speedy Prosecution (AHRC Case No. 4521 of 2003)

The complainant 'A', w/o 'B' of Nayagram village under Ramanikrishna T.E.P.O. in Karimganj district filled a complaint to the Commission stating that on the night of 20.05.2003 at about 12.30 p.m. some miscreants abducted her husband. She informed the Police of Nilambazar Police Station for tracing out her husband but no result came out.

Acting upon the case the Commission received 3 (three) reports from the Superintendent of Police, Karimganj, Assam[3]. From these reports the Commission found that on 20.5.2003 at about 2.20 A.M I/C Nilambazar Out Post received telephonic information from 'C' of Modan Mohan Tea Estate regarding the above abduction. The next day the complainant also filed a FIR. The Police started investigation and visited the place of occurrence and drew up a rough sketch map of the place of occurrence and arrested 9 (nine) persons. On 28.07.2003 the I/O of the case received telephonic information from the Deputy Superintendent of Police, (HQ) Karimganj, that on the intervening night the victim 'B' came back from the custody of Bangladesh based extremist group and was in the Barapunjee BSF Camp. They went to the said BSF camp and learnt that on 28.07.2003 in the morning a patrol party of BSF Dewtali found one person crossing the international border and entering Indian Territory from Bangladesh.

The *Naka* Party apprehended the person and brought him to the BSF camp for interrogation. On interrogation the victim informed that 'D', 'E', 'F', all of Barapnjee, along with some unknown extremist group kidnapped him. The I/O recorded the statement of 'B' u/s 161 Cr.P.C. and submitted a prayer for according prosecution sanction which had not yet been received.

The Commission received comments from the complainant. In her comment she accepted the report of the S.P. Karimganj but prayed for immediate sanction for prosecution.

In view of the above facts, the Commission recommended to the Superintendent of Police, Karimganj, to take up the matter with appropriate authority to grant sanction of the prosecution immediately so that they could proceed with the case.

Case No. 4

Suo-Motu Case on the Irregularities of District Jail of Nalbari (AHRC Case No. 4695 of 2003)

A news item under the caption "There are irregularities in the District Jail at Nalbari" appeared in the Assamese daily newspaper "The *Amar Asom*" on 1st of October, 2003. In the said news item it was mentioned that the inmates of the District Jail of Nalbari were deprived of medical treatment, drinking water and other necessities of life. It had also been alleged that there was corruption.

The Commission took *suo-motu* cognizance and called for a report from the Inspector General of Prison, Assam, Guwahati.

The Inspector General of Prisons had informed[4] the Commission that he had requested the Deputy Commissioner, Nalbari, to get the matter enquired into by an Executive Magistrate, accordingly 'A', Executive Magistrate, Nalbari, made an enquiry. The said enquiry report had been sent by the Deputy Commissioner, Nalbari,[5] to the Inspector General of Prisons who had forwarded the same to the Commission. The Commission found that the Executive Magistrate had visited the District Jail and talked to the inmates of the Jail and made other enquiries. According to the Executive Magistrate, inmates had been given tea and *chappati* in the morning, lunch in the afternoon and dinner in the evening. They were given non-vegetarian diet like fish, meat, eggs etc. twice in a week. The inmates also informed the Executive Magistrate that they were given good quality food. There was tube-well inside the Jail and there were filters installed. The inmates also informed that they had proper medical treatment whenever required. The barracks where the inmates are kept are being repaired also.

The Commission in the judgment accepted the report of the Executive Magistrate 'A' and hold that the news item was baseless.

Case No. 5

Case of Assault and Torture against Police (AHRC Case No. 4768/2003)

'A' of Juripar, Panjabari Road, Guwahati, filed a complaint petition before the Commission stating that on 18th Nov, 2003 at about 7.45 P.M. while he was busy in purchasing food items, he heard a loud sound and found that his scooter was dashed by a speeding Ambassador car which fled away towards Batahghuli. He followed the ambassador car and found 3 (three) occupants in the car who were police personnel. On query, all those persons attacked him and, thereafter, dragged him to the military campus of Narengi and continued to beat him mercilessly and accused him as a drunkard. He was subsequently taken to the Satgaon Police Station where they continued to torture him and he was not allowed to contact his relatives. Thereafter, he was shifted from Satgaon Police Station to Noonmati Police Station around midnight where he found his wife and some well wishers and, thereafter, he was taken to the Gauhati Medical College & Hospital by the police personnel for medical examination. Being aggrieved by the action of the police as above, he had then approached the Commission seeking redressal.

Acting on the said complaint, the Commission called for a report from the Superintendent of Police (City) Guwahati. Accordingly, the Superintendent of Police (City) Guwahati after an enquiry into the complaint sent report to the Commission. A copy of the report of the S.P. was sent to the complainant for his comments. The complainant also submitted his comments on the report. Thereafter, vide order dated 28.6.2005 the Commission directed the Director (Investigation) of the Commission to get the matter enquired into and, accordingly, the S.P (Investigation) 'B' after completion of the investigation submitted his report in which he concluded that ASI of Police 'C' of Satgaon Police Outpost violated the human rights of the complainant.

Accordingly the Commission issued a notice to ASI 'C', through the Sr. Superintendent of Police (City), Guwahati, asking him to show cause as to why appropriate recommendation was not made against him for alleged violation of human rights of the complainant. But ASI 'C' failed to submit his reply to the show cause notice and the case had to adjourned on as many as 9 (nine) occasions for non-receipt of his reply and, accordingly, the Commission proceeded with the case without having statements of ASI 'C' in reply to the show cause notice received by him.

While perusing the records of the case the commission found that the report of the Dy. Superintendent of Police, Chandmari Division, Guwahati admitted the assaults made on the complainant 'A' causing injury on his person. It had also been stated in the report that a case being Noonmati P.S Case No.464/2003 U/S 279/ 427/ 342/ 325/ 294/ 384 IPC was registered against UBC 'D' and H.G 'E' and, accordingly, 'D' was arrested and forwarded to Judicial custody while H.G 'E', surrendered before the Court. The enquiry report of the Superintendent of Police (Investigation) Cell of the Commission charged responsible ASI 'C', who was the In-charge of Satgaon Police Outpost at the relevant time for violation of human rights of the complainant 'A'. The fact established that the complainant 'A' sustained grievous injuries as a result of the assaults made on him. The medical prescriptions and the reports submitted by the complainant in the case had also lent support to his contention. The specific accusation of the complainant that he was assaulted by the Police/Home Guard personnel including 'C', In-charge of the Outpost stand un-rebutted as 'C' had failed to counter the allegations made by complainant despite receipt of the show cause notice issued to him and, accordingly the Commission accepted the report of the S.P (Investigation) Cell of the Commission 'B' as true and correct.

In its judgement order the Commission recommended for disciplinary action/proceeding against ASI 'C', the then In-charge of Satgaon Police Outpost should be launched by the Superintendent of Police, (City) Guwahati and also viewed that after completion of the disciplinary proceeding, the Authority may take necessary action according to law. The Commission did not recommended for any action against the UBC 'D' and Home Guard

'E' as a case had already been filed against them which will take its own course in accordance with law before the competent Court.

The Commission recommended that the Sr. Superintendent of Police, (City) Guwahati should submit compliance report to the Commission within a period of 6 (six) months from the date of receipt of the judgment order.

Case No. 6

Suo-motu Case of Negligence against Doctor and Nurse (AHRC Case No. 4947 of 2004)

The Commission took *suo-motu* cognizance on the basis of a news item under the caption "Sad demise of Mitali at Hospital" which appeared in the Assamese daily newspaper 'the Dainik Asom' on 26th April, 2004.

According to the said report, a girl aged about 13 years old, died at the Chhygaon, CHC, due to negligence of the Doctor. Mitali was a student of class VI and she was brought to the CHC at 1 P.M. She complained of vomiting and loose motion and the attending doctor prescribed medicines and also administered I.V. fluid. There was reaction due to I.V. Fluid. Due to exhaustion of the I.V. fluid the blood came out and fearing bad consequences the mother of the girl removed the saline bottle herself and informed the doctor. By the time the doctor came the girl died.

The Commission called for a report from the Director of Health Services, Assam. The Joint Director of Health Services got the matter enquired into by the Chief Medical & Health Officer (CD) and the Sub-Divisional Medical and Health Officer, P.H. Duty (Jointly). The enquiry report submitted by the Joint Director of Health Services, Kamrup, Guwahati[6] was forwarded[7] by the Addl. Director of Health Services, Assam, Hengrabari, Guwahati to the Commission.

The Enquiry Team examined 7 (seven) witnesses and observed that after the admission of the patient Dr. 'A' and ANM 'B' attended the patient and they started treatment immediately and I.V. infusion were given and after completion of the two bottles of I.V infusion no Doctor and Nurse attended the patient and the mother of the patient removed the I.V. infusion after she saw blood in the tube. It was also observed by the Enquiry Team that life of the patient could have been saved if the on duty doctor and nurse attended the patient at the very beginning of the rigor.

In view of the above report, the Commission issued show cause notices to Dr. 'A' and 'B', ANM.

Dr. 'A', Sr. M & HO, Chhaygaon CHC in reply to the show cause notice had admitted the death of Mitali. He stated that having diagnosed the aliment he prescribed the medicines and the nurse 'B' requested the parents of the patient to get these medicines from the market as these were not available in the CHC. Nurse 'B' carried out the advice of the Dr. 'A'. Duty of the nurse 'B' was till 2 P.M. therefore she left the CHE and her duty was taken over by another nurse. According to Dr. 'A' even after best available treatment the condition of the patient did not improve. 'B' informed Dr. 'A' about the signs of rigor on the patient. He immediately attended the patient and found that the rigor had indeed started after the infusion of I.V. drip No.3. Therefore, she asked the mother of the patient to immediately purchase a Decadran and avil injections from open market as these were not available in the CHE. 'B', the nurse left the Hospital as her duty was over. According to Dr. 'A' best possible and available treatment was offered by him with the help of another nurse 'C'. He further stated that other serious cases arrived at the CHC and one patient was having injury due to accident. As there was no other doctor he had no alternative but to attend the injured person. The nurse 'C' informed about the deteriorating condition of the patient, namely Mitalia. He rushed to her along with nurse 'C' and found that the mother of Mitali had removed the I.V. drip herself without even bothering to call the duty nurse. In spite of the best possible efforts the life of Mitali could not be saved. He further stated that the enquiry was conducted after 11 (eleven) months of occurrence and, therefore, the statements of the witnesses were bound to create confusion and contradiction. He further stated that nowhere in the Enquiry Report it was stated that the treatment of the patient was not initiated on time and that she was not attended to when she was brought to the CHC. There was no suggestion from the enquiry team as to any wrong diagnosis or treatment as given to the patient.

Regarding comments of the enquiry that no record was available Dr. 'A' had stated that Chhaygaon CHC was beneath 5ft of water during the flash flood that inundated the entire area in the year 2004. He had annexed a certificate from the Circle Officer Chhaygaon Revenue Circle.

'B', ANM, Chhaygaon CHC filed her reply to the show cause and she had taken the same stand as that of Dr. 'A'. She had also stated that her duty was over at 2 P.M. and after taking permission of Dr. 'A' she left the Hospital. The above two replies to the show-cause notices were sent to the Director of Health Services, Assam, Hengrabari for his views. According to the Director, Dr. 'A' was bound to be busy to attend the emergency case of accident and, therefore, it was presumed that there was no negligence on the part of Dr. 'A'. According to the Director, the Enquiry Report also did not mention of any wrong treatment.

In view of the above suggestion the Commission in the judgment order found that there was no negligence on the part of Dr. 'A' and Nurse 'B' and accordingly closed the case against the Doctor and the nurse.

Case No. 7

Case for Pay of Arrear, Pension and other Facilities of 'A' (AHRC Case NO.4970 of 2004)

'B' of Boiragimath, Dibrugarh, Assam, filed a complaint to the Commission and had stated that when she was going with her husband 'A' availing LTC in the year 1994 her husband went missing at the Bhusuwal Railway Station of Maharastha. Her husband was working as an UD Assistant in the Office of the Chief Medical & Health Officer, Dibrugarh. For the last 7 (seven) years she did not receive any communication from her husband. She applied to the concerned authority for arrear pay, pension and other benefits but no action was taken.

On that case the Commission had received letters from the Director of Health Services, Assam[8]. With that letter the Director of Health Services, Assam also forwarded letter of the Joint Director of Health Services, Dibrugarh[9]

From the above letters it appeared to the Commission that death certificate could not be prepared for not receiving the judgment of the Court. The complainant filed a Civil Suit being Title Suit No.102/05 before the Court of the Civil Judge No.1, (Junior Division) Dibrugarh and the suit was decreed on contest. The decree was dated 2nd May, 2006 and it was ordered that 'A', husband of the complainant/plaintiff, was declared to be dead. In the said suit the State of Assam and the Joint Director of Health Services, Dibrugarh and 3 (three) other persons were defendants and, therefore, decree was binding on the Joint Director of Health Services.

In view of the above order of the Court, the Commission in the judgment order recommended to the Director of Health Services, Assam and the Joint Director of Health Services, Dibrugarh to pay arrear salary, pension, family pension and other benefits within a period of 3 (three) months.

The complainant in her comments prayed that her daughter who was un-employed be appointed on compassionate ground. On that the Commission viewed that the complainant may file a proper petition before the appropriate authority and it would be considered and disposed off in accordance with law.

Case No. 8

Bullet Injury on 'A' by Police (AHRC Case No. 5010/2004)

'A' of Badarpur, Karmiganj district had lodged a complaint before the Commission stating, that on 12.3.2004 while he went to buy food articles in the market he became victim of Police firing. At that time while the Police resorted to firing on a procession, a shot pierced into his right leg and he fell down on the road. According to him, he was a poor daily labour and had to maintain his family consisting of 10 members and that due to the injury sustained by him he was not in a position to earn his livelihood.

Acting on the said complaint petition, the Commission called a report from the Superintendent of Police, Karimganj. Accordingly, a detailed report had been submitted by the S.P. Karimganj on receipt of which, the Commission sent a copy of the same to the complainant for his comments.

In his report, the S.P. Karmiganj had stated that on 12.03.2004 at 11.10 P.M. one 'A', son of Late 'B' of Alekhargool, P.S. Badarpur appeared at Badarpur P.S in an injured condition and, thereafter, he was sent to Badarpur Railway Hospital, Badarpur for treatment under escort. The Railway Hospital, Badarpur thereafter referred him to the Silchar Medical College & Hospital for better treatment. And on 14.3.2004 at 11.30 P.M. a complaint was lodged at Badarpur Police Station. During investigation, the I/O examined the victim and the complainant only, as other witnesses were not found available. The I/O also received the medical report in respect of the injury sustained by the injured 'A'. At the conclusion of the investigation the Police submitted F.R. in the case.

In his comments, the complainant 'A' had alleged that the Police personnel intentionally fired at him and, accordingly, he sustained injury over his right leg ankle as a result of which he became physically incapable and was not in a position to work properly. He also stated that he was admitted in the Silchar Medical College & Hospital on 13.3.2004 and he was treated there for about 1(one) month. He submitted one discharge certificate issued by the Silchar Medical College & Hospital wherein it was stated that he bore ballistic injury over right foot.

The Commission in the judgement order stated that it is clear that the complainant 'A' sustained bullet injury which was fired at him by the Police personnel as alleged by him. But in perusing all the reports the Commission found that the firing of bullet at the complainant 'A', causing injury to him was not intentional. However, as the complainant sustained the ballistic injury on his right foot as a result of the Police firing and was no material to show that at that particular point of time the complainant engaged himself in any unlawful activity as such, the Commission considered the view that the complainant was entitled to some amount of compensation. The complainant 'A' had also received an amount of Rs.10, 000/- (Rupees Ten thousand) only as compensation from the Hon'ble Chief Minister, Assam.

Although in his complaint, the complainant had also stated that he had already incurred an amount of Rs.17, 500/- only towards his treatment. Besides, he had also claimed to have lost his wages for 180 days at the rate of Rs.125/- per day. But as he had not submitted or placed on record any voucher including medical bills, cash memos etc in support of his claim the Commission recommended for awarding an amount of Rs.10, 000/- only as compensation. This money should be paid by Home & Political Department, Govt. of Assam through the Deputy Commissioner, Karimganj within a period of 4(four) months and compliance report thereof, should be submitted to the Commission by the Commissioner & Secretary, Home Department, Government of Assam in addition to the amount of Rs.10, 000/- only which he had already received from the Chief Minister, Assam.

Case No. 9

Suo-Motu Case on Torture in Police Custody (AHRC Case No.5050 of 2004)

The Commission took *suo-motu* cognizance on the basis of a news item which was published in the Assamese daily newspaper "the *Asomiya Pratidin*" on 29th July, 2004 under the caption "Inhuman torture by Lahowal Police: Third degree to 16 years aged Rahima".

According to the said newspaper report, Rahima Begum, daughter of Motiullah Ahmed of Bokel village under Lahowal P.S, was arrested on June 3rd, 2004 by Sri B. Deori, O/C, Lahowal Police Station, in connection with a theft case and was remanded to the Jail after subjecting her to inhuman torture. It was also alleged that she was handcuffed and tortured by S.I. Sri Deori, O/C, Lahowal Police Station and being unable to bear the torture she became senseless and had to be treated in the Jail. It was also alleged that Rohima was stripped and physically abused. The newspaper had also reported that Rahima also sustained wounds on her thighs, legs, hands and back which were shown to the media persons.

Acting upon the case the Commission received report from the District Magistrate, Dibrugarh[10]. The Deputy Commissioner got the matter enquired into by Smt Ruby Borah, Executive

Magistrate, Dibrugarh. The Deputy Commissioner had also received a report from the Superintendent of Police, Dibrugarh, which had also been sent to the Commission. The Superintendent of Police, Dibrugarh, by a separate letter[11] informed that an enquiry on the case was ordered through Shri A. Das, APS, Addl. Superintendent of Police (S) Dibrugarh and the said enquiry report had been sent.

Shri A. Das, APS, Addl. Superintendent of Police (S), Dibrugarh, Assam, had examined various witnesses including the victim and stated that the O/C, Lahowal P.S., on 2.6.2004 registered Lahowal P.S case No.70/04, u/s 380 IPC. An FIR was lodged by the complainant Sri Rajesh Shankar Rao Kunditji Girmee, Group Manager of Bokul T.E. stating that a theft of gold ornaments was committed in the Bunglow and during interrogation one Md. Salim Ahmed, servant of the complainant, admitted that he committed theft of the gold ornaments and gave them to one Lily Begam for sale. One gold chain was given to his sister Rahima Begum and another chain to his aunt Nagma Begum and, therefore, I/O arrested both Lily Begum and Rahima Begum who stated that the chain given to her was thrown to a nearby jungle.

Shri A. Das ultimately came to the conclusion that Rahima sustained minor injuries on her person during the period of her arrest and she was under treatment in the Central Jail, Dibrugarh, but no evidence could be collected regarding torture by S.I Deori in her private parts. Some injuries were also noticed by the Doctor. Therefore, Shri Das came to the conclusion that Miss Rahima sustained injuries while she was in police custody. Shri A. Das stated in his report that no direct evidence could be collected to establish the allegations of inhuman torture by S.I. B. Deuri but it was evident that Rahima sustained injuries while she was in police custody. Therefore, Addl. Superintendent of Police (S) Dibrugarh, Assam, held that S.I. Deori, the then O/C, Lahowal P.S. can be held responsible.

Ms. Ruby Borah, ACS, Executive Magistrate & Enquiry Officer, in her enquiry report had considered all the evidence collected by her, examined witnesses of 14 persons. She also examined 4 (four) documents. She had examined in detail the evidence recorded by her and, ultimately, came to the conclusion from the evidence recorded by her and documents examined by her and statements of victim, police personnel, Medical Officer etc, that Miss Rahima Begum was assaulted by S.I. B. Deori, the then O/C Lahowal P.S on legs, buttocks, thighs and hands during the period while she was in police custody but it could not be ascertained if Rahima was assaulted in her private parts.

Though the Addl. Superintendent of Police (S) had not found that S.I Deori, the then O/C Lahowal P.S, assaulted Miss Rahima but the Executive Magistrate clearly came to the finding that S.I. Deori, the then O/C Lahowal P.S, assaulted Rahima while she was in Police custody.

The Commission accepted both the reports and issued notice to show cause to S.I. B. Deori, the then O/C of Lahowal P.S. and Mr. Deori had filed the reply to the show cause notice. According to S.I Deori, he never assaulted Miss Rehima and the injuries on her body were prior to her arrest by the Police. He had also denied any harassment or torture by any Police personnel in the Police Station including himself and stated that she was kept under guard of a woman Police constable with other women UTPs. She was interrogated in presence of women Police constables and other police personnel at the Police Station. He had further stated that since 1990 he has been performing his duties very sincerely to the satisfaction of the superior officer and he was never suspended nor awarded any major or minor punishment nor any departmental proceeding had been drawn against him.

In view of the detailed enquiry reports by Ms. Ruby Borah, ACS, Executive Magistrate & Enquiry Officer and Sri A. Das, APS, Addl. Superintendent of Police (S), the Commission in its judgment order rejected the explanation given by S.I Deori in his reply to the show cause notice. However, considering his past record as stated by him in his reply to the show -cause the Commission opined that warning be given to S.I Deori for assaulting Miss Rahima Begum. The Commission also awarded an interim compensation of Rs.10, 000/- (Rupees Ten Thousand) only to Miss Rahima Begum. The Commission recommended that this amount be paid by the Home Department, Govt. of Assam, within a period of 3 (three) months from the date of judgment order.

Case No. 10

Suo-Motu Case on the Report published in 'the Sentinel' "People Urge AHRC to Summon State Government" (AHRC Case No. 5079 of 2004)

The Commission took *suo-motu* cognizance by order dated 21.08.2004 on the basis of a news item under the caption "People Urge AHRC to Summon State Government" published on 21.08.2004 in the local English Daily "The Sentinel".

As per the report, after the bomb blast at Dhemaji Parade ground on the Independence Day several people including children were killed and fear psychosis continued to prevail among the people of Dhemaji district who were yet to recover from the shock of the deadly terrorist attack.

The Superintendent of Police, the Addl. Superintendent of Police and the Deputy Commissioner, Dhemaji, were transferred after the said terrorist attack. The people urged the Commission to interfere in the matter. It was also reported that only because of loopholes in the security system innocent people mostly children had to lose their lives.

The Commission had received report from the Deputy Commissioner, Dhemaji[12]. This letter showed that the Deputy Commissioner, Dhemaji wrote a letter[13] to the Superintendent of Police that construction and other works of the Dhemaji College Field were completed for the Independence Day celebration and he was requested to take charge of the field for ceremonial flag hoisting. He had given a detailed report regarding security arrangement.

From the letter[14] of the Political (A) Department the Commission found that the Government had appointed one man enquiry committee headed by Shri P.C. Sarma, IAS Addl. Chief Secretary, Assam, to enquire into the incident on bomb blast.

As the Government had already constituted a Committee to enquire into the matter the Commission decided not to go into this aspect of the matter. Now the question before the Commission was whether proper treatment was given to the injured children. The Commission called for a report from the District Medical & Health Officer, Dhemaji by order dated 02.12.2004. In spite of reminders/requests no report was received from the District Medical & Health Officer, Dhemaji. The Commission issued summons for personal appearance of the District Medical & Health Officer, Dhemaji, by order dated 18.01.2006. The Joint Director of Health Services, Dhemaji, Dr. B. Pegu personally appeared before the Commission on 24.08.2006 and also filed a report[15]. Due to non-receipt of report on time, the case was pending for long time.

From the report of the Joint Director of Health Services, Dhemaji, the Commission found that due to the bomb blast by the extremists on 15th August,2004 13 (thirteen) numbers of persons died and all the injured persons in the bomb blast were shifted to the Civil Hospital without delay. Next day most of the children came to the Hospital with Trauma and some of them were treated as outdoor patients. All the patients admitted in the Civil Hospital were examined by psychiatrists and psychologists who came from the Assam Medical College and Hospital, Dibrugarh. Apart from them a team of Doctors were engaged to follow up the patients discharged from the Civil Hospital to their home. Different meetings were held at the different places where psychological treatment was imparted to the community by the specialists.

In view of the above report, the Commission in the judgment order opined proper medical treatment/advice was given to the victims of the bomb blast.

Case No. 11

Suo-Motu Case on Custodial Death and Three Persons Killing in Police Firing (AHRC Case No. 5080 of 2004)

On the basis of two news items which appeared on 21st and 22nd August, 2004 in the 'Assam Tribune', local English daily, the Commission took *suo-motu* cognizance.

In the news item published on 21st August, 2004 under the caption 'Custodial death', it was stated that one Raseswar Hokai was picked up by police for his suspected ULFA links. Thereafter, he was allegedly tortured by police as later on he was found dead at Ulukunchi Police Outpost under Baithalangsu Police Station in Karbi Anglong district, Assam. The news item which appeared in the said newspaper dated 22nd August, 2004 it was stated "3 persons were killed in Baithalangsu Police firing" while an irate mob '*gheraoed*' Ulukunchi Police Outpost.

Subsequently, the General Secretary of All Tiwa Students' Union (ATSU), the General Secretary of Tiwa Sahitya Sabha and the General Secretary of All Tiwa Women Association (ATWA) Central Committee, Morigaon, Assam, submitted a memorandum before the Commission giving full facts of both the incidents.

The Commission called for a report from the Deputy Commissioner, Karbi Anglong who forwarded two enquiry reports, the post mortem reports, the inquest reports[16] etc. The Inspector General of Police (OSD) I/C Human Rights Cell, Assam Police (HQs) Ulubari, Guwahati-5 also forwarded the detailed report on the case[17], the inquest report, the post mortem report, the magisterial enquiry report and the copy of the letter[18] of the Superintendent of Police, Karbi Anglong, Diphu.

On the basis of the Magisterial Enquiry Report, the Commission issued show cause notices to ASI K. Brahma and Constable No.95 Jaymangal Singh and they submitted their replies to their respective show cause notices to the Commission.

Mr. T.T.D. Daulaguphu, ACS, Executive Magistrate, Hamren, Karbi Anglong district, had submitted two enquiry reports, namely report of the circumstances leading to death of Radeshwar Kangkai, son of Guneswar Kangkai of Ulukunchi village under Baithalangso P.S, who died in Police custody on 20.8.2004 and the report on the circumstances leading to orders for firing where 3(three) persons were killed at Ulukunchi P.P. area on 20.8.2004. The Commission had perused both the reports and found that Mr. T.T.D. Daulaguphu, ACS, Executive Magistrate, Hamren Karbi Anglong district after examining all the witnesses had given his findings. The Commission accepted both the reports.

I. Regarding Death of Radeshwar Hukai

Mr. Daulaguphu after examining all the evidence recorded by him and perusing other documents came to the findings that on 20.8.2004 I/C of the P.P. ASI Khudiram Brahma at about 5.30 A.M. along with C/95 Constable Jaymangal Singh went to the shop of Paban Chandra Ingti and thereafter, picked up Radeshwar Hukai and took him to the Police Station for interrogation for his suspected ULFA links. Both the Police officials were in civil dress. Nothing incriminating was found against Hukai. I/C ASI K. Brahma took Hukai to the Police Out Post. He was handcuffed and taken out towards the village at about 7 A.M. ASI Brahma started beating mercilessly Radeshwar Hukai with a wooden baton on his back, arms and legs. Constable Jaymangal Singh also kicked him on the chest. Many people were eyewitnesses to Radeshwar Hukai being beaten by the I/C. According to Mr. Daulaguphu, the arrest of Radeshwar Hukai was unjustified and he was tortured by ASI Brahma who was helped by Constable Jaymangal Singh. Mr. Daulaguphu noted that as per the Inquest Report there were injuries on the body of the deceased Radheshwar Hukai. Even other constables who were present at the Police Out Post at that point of time also saw that Radheshwar Hukai was tortured and beaten by ASI Brahma. Mr. Daulaguphu noted that according to the post mortem report, the death was due to respiratory arrest following spinal injuries. The post mortem report also indicated two injuries on the back and one on the spinal cord. Mr. Daulaguphu also noted that arrest memo was not given. This was a clear violation of the directions of the Hon'ble Supreme Court. Mr. Daulaguphu came to the findings that I/C ASI Khudiram Brahma was guilty of arresting and torturing Radheshwar Hukai as a of which the victim died. He suggested that legal action be taken immediately against ASI K. Brahma and Constable Jaymangal Singh for assisting the I/C ASI Brahma on the arrest and torture of Radeshwar Hukai.

II. Regarding Police Firing Resulting in the Death of 3 (Three) Persons

Mr. Daulaguphu came to the finding that firing was justified as the crowd was un-controllable and damage caused to the PP and there was danger to life of police personnel who took shelter in the Police Outpost. However, he was of the opinion that firing was not at all controlled and firing of 85 rounds was too much in excess of what was required on that day. Therefore, the firing was not a controlled one, it was rather indiscriminate. Mr. Daulaguphu also noted that Tong Mithi got a bullet entry mark on the back side and exit mark on the front. This showed that the person was hit while he was fleeing from the place of occurrence. According to Mr. Daulaguphu, some persons instigated the crowd to cause damage to the Police Station. Mr. Daulaguphu, ACS, had also sent photographs of the Police Outpost and this showed that crowd damaged the properties of the Police Out Post extensively. Therefore, he suggested that legal action should be initiated against the instigators, namely (1) Sri Augustin Phujong and (2) Sri Prabin Maslaï.

From the report of the Superintendent of Police, Karbi Anglong, the Commission found that one police proceeding had already been started against Shri Augustin Phujong and Shri Prabin Maslai in connection with Baithalangso P.S Case No.39/ 2004. According to the Superintendent of Police, Karbi Anglong, both the persons were evading arrest. Another case was registered, namely Baithalangsu P.S Case No.04/2005 u/s 302/34 I.P.C against ASI K. Brahma and Constable No.95 Jaymangal Singh.

In reply to the show cause notice ASI K. Brahma stated that when Radeshwar Hukai was in police custody he complained of some health problem and medical treatment was given but his life could not be saved. This point was examined and rejected by the Magistrate Mr. Daulaguphu. ASI K. Brahma denied that he went in plain clothes and without wearing uniform to the house of the deceased Radeshwar Hukai. The Commission had gone through the show cause reply and rejected the same. The constable Jaymangal Singh had denied the allegations that were brought against him. He had stated the same thing as stated by ASI K. Brahma regarding the health problem of deceased Radeshwar Hukai. He had also denied that he went in a civil dress to the house of the deceased Hukai and also the allegations of torture.

The Commission rejected the explanations given by the two police personnel in view of the comprehensive and exhaustive report of Mr. Daulaguphu. In the judgment order the Commission viewed that this was a case of clear violation of human rights of deceased Radheswar Hukai and his next of kin is entitled to get appropriate interim compensation. Accordingly, the Commission awarded a sum of Rs.1,00,000/- (Rupees One Lakh) only to be paid to the next of kin of deceased Radeshwar Hukai by the Home & Political Department, Govt. of Assam through the Deputy Commissioner, Karbi Anglong, Diphu within a period of 4(four) months from the date of judgment order.

As the police firing was uncontrolled and rather indiscriminate the Commission also opinioned that the next of the kin of the 3 (three) victims who were killed in police firing, namely Tong Mithi (23 years) En Lumphoi (55 yrs) and Khamar Pumah (70 yrs) were entitled for interim compensation.

The Commission recommend that a sum of Rs. 1,00,000/- (Rupees One lakh) only shall be paid as interim compensation to the next of kin of deceased Tong Mithi, a sum of Rs.70,000/- (Rupees Seventy thousand) only to the next of kin of deceased En Lumphoi and a sum of Rs.50,000/- (Rupees Fifty thousand) only to the next of kin of Khamar Pumah shall be paid by the Home & Political Department, Govt. of Assam within a period of 4 (four) months from the date of judgment order.

As per the suggestions of Mr. Daulaguphu for the arrest, torture and death of deceased Radeshwar Hukai a case had been started, namely Baithalangsu P.S Case No.04/2005 u/s 302/34 I.P.C against ASI K. Brahma and constable No.95 Jaymangal Singh so the Commission did not suggest any departmental proceeding but as per the guidelines of the National Human Rights Commission the Commission recommended that for the investigation of the case either by the CID Department or by a Police Officer of some other district. Accordingly, the Commission recommended the Director General of Police, Assam, to take appropriate action.

Case No. 12

Ill-treatment of Female inmates by a Nurse in the Dibrugarh Central Jail (AHRC Case No. 5160 of 2004)

About 13 (thirteen) female inmates of the Dibrugarh Central Jail had filed a complaint petition to the Commission alleging that Smt Kakoli Das Gupta, a nurse of the Central Jail Dibrugarh, looked down upon them and ill-treated them. They stated that she never attended the Hospital before 10 a.m. and always left the Hospital before 11 a.m. They also alleged about negligence of duty on her part as a result of which the inmates of the Jail had to suffer.

The Executive Magistrate, who conducted an enquiry on that, after examining inmates and other persons, opined that Smt Kakali Dasgupta, was an arrogant, negligent staff of the Jail and her attitude towards her duty was most unbecoming. There was no dedication on her part for her job as a nurse.

The Commission also got the comments of the inmates of the jail who have filed the complaint petition.

In view of the above facts, the Commission took serious note of the conduct of Smt Kakoli Das Gupta, her misbehavior towards the jail inmates and lack of dedication towards her duty. The Commission in the judgment order opined that a nurse should be more careful while treating the inmates of the Jail as they are always mentally disturbed persons. The Commission recommended to the Director of Health Services, Assam, to immediately transfer Smt Kakoli Das Gupta and if necessary, he could take action against her.

Case No. 13

Suo-Motu Case of *Lathi* Charge in Constables Recruitment (AHRC Case No. 5178 of 2004)

The Commission took *suo-motu* cognizance in this case on a news item which appeared in almost all the newspapers of Assam on 4.12.2004. According to the said news item, during recruitment of police constables, candidates were subjected to *lathi*-charge as a result of which some candidates got severe injury and a candidate died at Nalbari. The recruitment tests were conducted at various places of Assam. The Commission called for a report from the Director General of Police, Assam.

The Inspector General of Police, (OSD) & I/C Human Rights Cell, Assam Police (HQs) Ulubari, Guwahati[19] had sent the report received from the Superintendent of Police, Nalbari. The IGP also sent a letter[20] and two reports.

From the letter of the IGP dated 1st Feb, 2005 the Commission came to know that except the S.P (City), Guwahati and the S.P, Nalbari, other Superintendents of Police had denied any *lathi* charge or death during the recruitment process.

From the report of the Superintendent of Police, Nalbari[21] the Commission found that recruitment for the post of police constables was held at 14th AP Bn HQ Daulasal under Nalbari district where about 17/18 thousand candidates including their guardians assembled in front of the main gate causing blockage of vehicular traffic on the PWD Road. The police personnel including the CRPF who were on duty made all efforts to maintain law and order by announcement through loudspeaker time and again for maintaining peace and tranquility and to clear the road. At about 11 A.M. the crowd became violent and tried to enter into the field by force through the main gate. The police personnel who were present tried to persuade and control them but some miscreants from the crowd threw stones on police personnel as result of which three police personnel received injuries. Another attempt was made to maintain law and order but the crowd again became violent and the police had to use mild *lathi*-charge. The crowd was controlled and the interview was completed. Accordingly Mukalmua P.S Case No.95/04 was registered. No casualty or injury was reported from the crowd including the candidates and their relatives. On the same day at about 4.30 P.M. an accident took place at Bortola on Hajo-Daulasal PWD road at a distance of about 8 K.M. from the 14th AP Bn Headquarters and one person died on the spot. A police case was also registered. On previous day i.e. 2.12.2004 another accident took place at Chanda near Mukalmua on Hajo Daulasal PWD road at a distance of 4 K.M. west from the Mukalmua P.S where one person died on the spot and it had no connection with the recruitment rally.

The Superintendent of Police (City) Guwahati had informed[22] the Commission that recruitment for the posts of constable was held at two places, namely 4th AP Bn HQ, Kahilipara and 10th AP Bn H.Q., Kahilipara on 3.12.2004. In the morning there were huge gatherings at both the recruitment centres and about 18,000 candidates gathered in front of the main gate at 4th AP Bn (HQ). About two thousand candidates were allowed to enter the parade field for physical test. There were about 15,000-16,000 candidates outside the main gate demanding entry into the parade field. As there was no space for more candidates they were informed that they may be allowed to enter after completion of the first stage. In spite of repeated requests, some miscreants from the crowd started pelting stones as a result of which six constables sustained injuries on their persons. The candidates were informed that recruitments would continue for several days and each and every candidate would be allowed to appear in the fitness test. The candidates at this stopped creating nuisance and they remained outside the main gate. According to the Superintendent of Police, City, Guwahati, there was a rumour outside the main gate that few candidates sustained injury due to stampede while entering the parade field by breaking the gate of 4th AP Bn but no such injured candidate was found. The local hospitals and nursing homes were also verified to ascertain the truth but the police authority was informed that no such injured person was admitted for treatment. One girl fell unconscious in the crowd and she was given medical treatment in the 4th AP Bn and was released later on. There was no *lathi*-charge.

From the above report the Commission in the judgment order mentioned that the Commission was satisfied that police did not resort to unnecessary *lathi*-charge or that any candidate died in the process. But the Commission was unhappy that huge number of candidates as 17,000-18,000 appeared in the recruitment test. The Commission suggested to the Director General of Police, Assam, that in future while recruiting persons for the posts of constable, efforts should be made that number of candidates called for fitness test be kept to minimum and that proper arrangement be made for drinking water, shades for taking rest and medical faculties etc.

Case No. 14

Complaint Petition by 'A' and 'B' (HIV Positive) forwarded by Smt Jahnabi Goswami, General Secretary of Assam Network of Positive People (ANP+) (AHRC Case No. 5262 of 2005)

'A' and 'B' of Namrup in Dibrugarh district filed a complaint which was forwarded by Smt Jahnabi Goswami, General Secretary of Assam Network of Positive People (ANP+), Sundarpur, Guwahati.

The complainant stated that on 1.12.2004 they were invited by the Councilor of Dibrugarh V.C.T.C on the Worlds AIDS Day. When they reached there at 10.30 A.M. they waited for some time. Thereafter, Dr. 'C' of the Pathology Department, Assam Medical College & Hospital, along with 4(four) other persons entered into the room and started asking questions as to when and how they got HIV Positive. They saw a video camera in the hand of a person and Dr. 'C' told them that they would take one photograph and send it to the Chief Minister and the Health Minister so that they would get some assistance from the Government to which they agreed as they were poor. On the following day they saw news items in two daily newspapers, namely 'the Telegraph' and the 'Dainik Janambhoomi' regarding their previous day discussion. It was also beamed in the NE Television with their photograph without giving their names. The complainants were HIV Positive for last 3 (three) years and they could not work. The complainant 'A' had a betel nut shop in front of their house. Their son at that time was studying in Sishu Niketan School, Namrup, Dibrugarh. It was alleged in the complaint that after the publication of the news item the school teacher did not allow the son of the complainants to enter the school premises as he was HIV positive. The customers also stopped coming to his shop. On receipt of the above two complaints, the Commission called for a report from the principal, Assam Medical College & Hospital, Dibrugarh and the secretary, Assam Aids Control Society, Khanapara, Guwahati and also from Dr. 'C' of the pathology department, Assam, Medical College & Hospital, Dibrugarh.

Dr. 'C' in her comments denied all the allegations. According to her, the two complainants 'A' and 'B' met her on 1st December, 2004 in her duty room of the Assam Medical College & Hospital and talked to her. They informed that the Councilor of V.C.T.C invited both of them to participate in the World AIDS day programme which was held at the Central Jail, Dibrugarh. She accompanied them to the room of the Councilor and during conversation with them they informed her about their desire to identify themselves in the society and live a meaningful life like Smt Jahanabi Goswami. She left the room of the Councilor and after about half an hour again went to the Councilor's room where she saw many persons. She recognized 'D' reporter of the newspaper "The Telegraph" and asked him why he was present. 'D' replied that 1st of December is AIDS day, and, thereafter, he went to the room of the Councilor to collect information. 'D' also met the above two complainants and they were talking. Dr. 'C' specifically told newspaper reporters not to publish the names of the complainants. Thereafter, she went to the Central Jail, Dibrugarh, for the World AIDS Day programme and found that the above two complainants were actively participating in the above programme.

The Principal, Assam Medical College & Hospital, Dibrugarh, enquired into the matter and stated that the Councilor did not call the complainants for press interview. He had also forwarded written statements of Dr. 'C' and the Councilors of VCTC[23]. From the report of the Councilors the Commission found that some media people (both Press & T.V) gathered there to take photographs but they were told not to take photograph in the room as it was illegal.

The Commission also received the report[24] from the Project Director, Assam State AIDS Control Society, Khanapara, Guwahati. Some relevant portions of the report are noted down here –

The Project Director, Assam State AIDS Control Society met

the Principal 'E' The Principal agreed to readmit the child and also to arrange a separate class for the child.

After the intervention programmes conducted by the health officials and NGOs the social status of the family had improved. Friends and relatives were then visiting the family.

The NGOs also contacted the District Elementary Education Officer for the purpose of readmission of the child.

The NGO, SEWA, extended financial assistance to the affected family to meet the expenses required in connection with treatment. 'A', the father of the child, was admitted in Gauhati Medical College Hospital, in a general ward along with other general patients for treatment. The required medicines were provided observing his health status.

Smt Jahnabi Goswami, General Secretary, Principal, had given comments on the report of the Assam State AIDS Control Society, Khanapara, Guwahati. The Commission accepted the following recommendations made by the Principal:-

a) We would like to recommend that in regard to the child readmission into the school we would have to aware the parents of the children reading in that particular school because it had been mentioned in the ASACS letter that parents were arrogant in readmitting the child in that school. If ASACS wanted then we could take the responsibility of organizing such kind of awareness programmes. If we were unable to do that then the whole concept of awareness would be in dustbin and we would never been able to create awareness in the society. We thought that this problem would be solved very easily with a strong awareness drive throughout the community.

b) If ASACS would have maintained GIPA (Greater Involvement of People Living with HIV/AIDS) then the process of creating awareness would have been easier. From the next time if any such kind of situation come up then they should maintain GIPA first.

c) In order to eradicate stigma & discrimination associated with HIV positive both the NGO, school should work together.

d) Due to the paucity of fund the school was unable to visit frequently the places like Namrup, no matter how much hard they try to mobilize fund. Therefore it was recommended that if ASACS could allocate separate fund for purpose this would go a long way in meeting the present challenges.

The Commission accordingly, recommended that the Project Director, Assam State AIDS Control Society, Khanapara, Guwahati, would consider the suggestions of Smt Jahnabi Goswami and implement it.

In the judgment of the case the Commission accepted the comments of Dr. 'C' and opined that she was not responsible for the Press reports which appeared in the newspapers and which were also telecasted by the NE T.V.

Case No. 15

Case on the Collapse of Sivsagar Jail Wall (AHRC Case No. 5475/2005)

This case had been registered on the basis of a newspaper report under the caption "Wall of Sivasagar Jail collapsed" published in the Assamese daily newspaper 'the Agradoot' dated 25.7.2005.

As per the newspaper report, a portion of the large wall on the northeast side of the Sivasagar Jail collapsed at 8.20 A.M. on 24.7.2005. According to the report, immediately after the collapse of the wall the authority posted Police personnel to guard the collapsed portion of the wall and the broken portion of the wall was being protected by C.I sheets. It had been alleged that the wall of the Jail which was constructed in the year 1932 collapsed as a result of non-repair of the jail since its construction.

The Commission while taking cognizance of the case on the basis of the newspaper report was constrained to note that the wall of the jail collapsed because of sheer negligence on the part of the jail authorities and there could have been law and order problem if the prisoners in the jail had taken the opportunity of fleeing the jail through the broken portion wall.

Acting on the aforesaid news item, detailed reports were called by the Commission from Deputy Commissioner, Sivasagar and the Inspector General of Prisons, Assam. They were also directed to indicate in the report as to the steps taken to construct the broken portion of the wall permanently and also to construct the whole wall which was reportedly in bad shape so that escape of prisoners from the jail in future could be permanently averted.

Accordingly, the Commission received reports of the Deputy Commissioner, Sivasagar and the Inspector General of Prisons, Assam which was forwarded to the Commission by the Under Secretary to the Government of Assam, Political Department. In his report the Inspector General of Prisons, Assam, Smt R. Kalita, ACS stated that the collapsed portion of the north-side (rear) enclosures wall of the District Jail, Sivasagar had already been permanently re-constructed through the PWD at the cost of Rs.4,75,905/-. The re-construction had been done with pile foundation for securing greater strength and durability of the wall. It had also been stated that steps had been taken for re-construction of the wall of the jail (excluding the collapsed portion which is already re-constructed) as a part of renovation of Sivasagar District Jail under the ongoing scheme of modernization of Prison Administration which was implemented with Central assistance on 75 : 25 cost sharing basis. The above scheme of modernization of Prison Administration was a five year scheme and allocation of Rs.24.00 Lakhs had been earmarked in the 4th Annual Action Plan of the scheme. The Addl. Deputy Commissioner, Sivasagar in his report also stated that the re-construction of the broken portion of the boundary wall of Sivasagar jail had already been completed during the month of February, 2006.

After going through the above mentioned reports the Commission hoped and trusted that the authority concerned would take effective steps to expedite completion of the construction of the walls of the Jail within the stipulated time.

Under the above circumstances, the Commission felt that it had nothing more to do on the case.

Case No. 16

Case of Custodial Death 'A' (AHRC Case No. 5690 of 2006)

The Commission received a WT Message No.SVR/V/06/143 dated 15.1.2006 from the Superintendent of Police, Sivasagar. The W.T. Message was addressed to the National Human Rights Commission, New Delhi.

According to this message, the S.P. informed the Commission that on the intervening night of 14.01.2006 and 15.01.2006 at about 1 A.M. S.I. 'B' of Sivasagar Police Station, who was on night patrol duty on the night, found one unknown person loitering suspiciously at *Babu Patty* Road, Sivasagar town. On interrogation the said person disclosed his name and address as 'A', son of 'C' of Old D.C. Bunglow Road, Dibrugarh and stated the he was looking for a PCO. He could not give satisfactory account to the Police Officer for his presence in the area at the dead of night. He was taken to the Police Station for verification. At the Police Station S.I. 'B' intimated the matter to 'D', the brother-in-law of 'A'. 'D' informed the Police that 'A' had a quarrel with his wife over some domestic affairs and left the house the same night after assaulting his father-in-law 'E', father of 'D'. The message also stated that 'A' was also found imbalanced in talking. He complained of chest pain and, therefore, he was shifted to the Sivasagar Civil Hospital and admitted at 1.15 a.m. Thereafter, he was declared dead.

The Commission had received the enquiry report of the Addl. District Magistrate, Sivasagar, the inquest report and the post mortem report sent by the Deputy Commissioner, Sivasagar[25]. According to the post mortem report, there was no injury on the body of the deceased but the surgeon could not give his opinion regarding the cause of death in absence of forensic report.

The District Magistrate, who conducted the enquiry, got the forensic report and the report gave negative test for a common poison. According to the enquiry report, detention of 'A' in the Sivasagar Police Station in the early hours of 15.1.2006 appeared to be unwanted. After the confirmation of identity he should have been handed over to the family or he should have been released from the police station without detaining him unnecessarily.

The Commission in the judgment report viewed that the Commission was unable to agree with the enquiry report in as much as the deceased was found loitering in late night and he was behaving unnaturally. It concluded that his death did not take place due to Police torture and, therefore, the Commission opined that, it was a case of natural death.

The Commission also stated that it took cognizance of the case on 17.1.2006 and NHRC did so on 30.1.2006. As the AHRC took cognizance earlier than the NHRC, it took up the case and accordingly informed the NHRC.

The Commission in the judgment order held that there was no violation of human rights.

Case No. 17

Death of son of 'A' for negligence of ASEB (AHRC case No. 5831 of 2006)

'A' of Valley View, Rongkhelan, Ward No.8, Karbi Anglong, filed a complaint to the Commission stating that on 24.06.2005 at about 1.30 P.M. a high voltage electrical wire fell down on his son who was aged 18 years and was killed. According to the complainant, the high tension overhead wire started sparkling since the last 3 (three) days before the incident occurred and the matter was reported to the ASEB Diphu on time. The incident took place just outside the boundary of the ASEB Divisional (Control Room) and the sparkling wire was visible from the ASEB Colony, Diphu, but nothing was done by the Department.

The Commission sought report from the Deputy Commissioner, Karbi Anglong at Diphu and the Commission received report[26] and the Deputy Commissioner had forwarded the reports of the S.P, Karbi Anglong, Diphu and the Deputy General Manager, KANCH Electric Circle, CAEDCL, Diphu.

The Deputy General Manager (HR), O/O the Managing Director, CAEDCL, Bijuli Bhawan, Paltanbazar, Guwahati-1 had forwarded the enquiry report of the Deputy Chief Electrical Inspector –cum- Advisor, Govt. of Assam. The Deputy Manager had informed the Commission that the ASEB was not agree with the findings of the enquiry report and had stated that a thatched house was constructed unauthorizedly under the High Tension 11 KV line about 15 years after the 11 KV line (industry feeder) was commissioned without obtaining any permission either from the Municipality Authority or from the local ASEB authority.

According to the report of the Dy. Chief Electrical Inspector-cum-Adviser, Govt. of Assam the accident occurred due to snapping and detachment of live conductor from the pin insulator fixed on the pole, which got punctured. The so detached live line fell and was lying on the thatched house in a hanging position, to which, the victim unknowingly came in contact and got electrocuted. And the lightning arrestor installed at the 33/11 KV sub-station did not respond to the lightning stroke.

Further the report said that no circuit breaker was installed at the sending end of the said 11 KV line for protection at the 33/11 KV sub-station, instead, only Drop- Out Fuse Assembly was used for the high voltage overhead line, which did not act in any situation other than rated over current. As such after snapping of one phase conductor of the line and subsequently coming in contact with the thatched house, no protection acted and the conductor in issue remained in live condition, leading to electrocution of the victim.

On the basis of the facts and circumstances leading to the accident the report said that there occurred contravention of the provisions of rule 29, 64(A) (2) & 91 of the Indian Electricity Rules, 1956 on part of the owner of the 11 KV high voltages overhead electric transmission line in issue, i.e. the Assam State Electricity Board.

The report recommended that the safety provisions as mentioned in the Indian Electricity Rules, 1956 should be strictly complied with by the supplier of electricity and all line and sub-station equipments should be maintained in safe condition.

Thus, from the said report the Commission found that there was negligence on the part of the ASEB. Accordingly, they were responsible for the death of young boy. Therefore the Commission recommended for the payment of compensation of Rs.80, 000/- (Rupees Eighty thousand only) to the legal heirs of Late 'B' within a period of 3 (three) months from the date of receipt of the judgment order. The amount should be paid by the ASEB to the Deputy Commissioner, Karbi Anglong, Diphu, who would disburse the amount to the legal heirs of the above deceased person.

Case No. 18

Harrasment case of 'A' (AHRC Case No. 5879 of 2006)

'A', wife of 'B' of Pachatia village under Morigaon P.S of Morigaon district, filed a complaint to the Commission with the allegation that she was working as Asst. Teacher in Morigaon H.S & M.P School and her husband, who was a Branch Manager of LIC, was posted at Jharkhand. She was staying alone with her 4 years old daughter in a rented house at Morigaon. According to her, taking advantage of the absence of her husband she had been variously harassed by 'C', Lower Division Assistant of Morigaon H.S and M.P. School, 'D', wife of 'C', 'E', brother of 'C' and 'F', a Lower Division Assistant in the Office of the Inspector of Schools, Morigaon. She had further alleged that 'C' and 'F' even went to the extent of enticing her to fulfil their evil desires. But as they failed to do so, on the night 9.6.2006 at about 1 A.M. 'C' with another unknown person forcibly entered her house and tried to harass her sexually. When she shouted for help they fled away. After that she filed an FIR at Morigaon P.S. but the Police did not take any action. She also alleged that on 13-6-2006 about 9-30 A.M. while she was going to school she was assaulted by 'D', wife of 'C'.

The Commission sought report from S.P., Morigaon and accordingly received report[27]. The S.P. in the report stated that the complainant filed an FIR at Morigaon P.S. stating about the incident on 13-6-2006. On the same day about 8.35 AM 'D', wife of 'C', also filed a complaint against the complainant. And from the enquiry it was found that the parties are working in the same school and they had long standing enmity between them. In order to ensure that no untoward incident takes place between the two parties in near future a non FIR case u/s 107 Cr.P.C had been registered and after submission of the non FIR case, no further incident of quarrel had occurred between the two parties. The S.P. further stated that at that time there was no threat to life of 'A' and adequate preventive precautionary measures were being taken by police.

The Commission also received a report from Inspector of Schools, Morigaon[28]. The Inspector of Schools in the report had given the back ground of the parties and also stated that the incident took place beyond office hours.

The Commission also found that complainant in her comments on the report of S.P. had stated that after filing the case there was an attempt to compromise the case and for that meeting was held on 29th August, 2006. In the meeting a suggestion was made on the matter to which the complainant agreed. Therefore she did not want to proceed with the case.

In view of the above position, the Commission found that there was no necessity for further orders. Accordingly the Superintendent of Police, Morigaon, Inspector of Schools, Morigaon and the complainant were informed and the case was closed.

Manipur Human Rights Commission (MHRC)

So far as the powers, functions and working of the MHRC are concerned it is not very different from AHRC. From the records available at the office of the MHRC it is seen that it gives emphasis on enquiring into the cases of violation of human rights in order to ensure and promote the rights of the people of Manipur.

Table 3.3: Statement of Cases between 1999[29] and 31st December 2007

i)	Total number of cases registered	:	1163
ii)	Total number of cases disposed off	:	599
iii)	Total number of Rape cases registered	:	94
iv)	Total number of Rape cases disposed off	:	12
v)	No. of custodial death cases registered	:	7

Source: Office of the Manipur Human Rights Commission

Table 3.4
Year-wise Statement of Cases

Year	*Total Number of Cases Registered*	*Total Number of Cases Disposed*
1999	202	127
2000	108	38
2001	192	112
2002	186	47
2003	138	113
2004	109	65
2005	116	73
2006	48	17
2007	64	7

Source: Office of the Manipur Human Rights Commission

From the above chart it is evident that maximum number of cases were registered and disposed in the beginning of MHRC. However, after the initial enthusiasm the numbers of cases registered and disposed started decreasing. Another important thing is that in the initial years the gap between cases registered and disposed off is very low. As for example, in 1999 and 2001 out of the total cases registered 62.87% cases and 58.33% cases were disposed off respectively. But in 2006 and 2007 the percentage of cases disposed off stood at 35.41% and 10.93% respectively. Such a situation casts negative image so far as the working of the MHRC is concerned.

Selective Cases

Similar to the AHRC in case of the MHRC also study of cases will give us some idea about how the Commission has been handling the cases since its inception. Source of the cases are case files collected from Manipur Human Rights Commission.

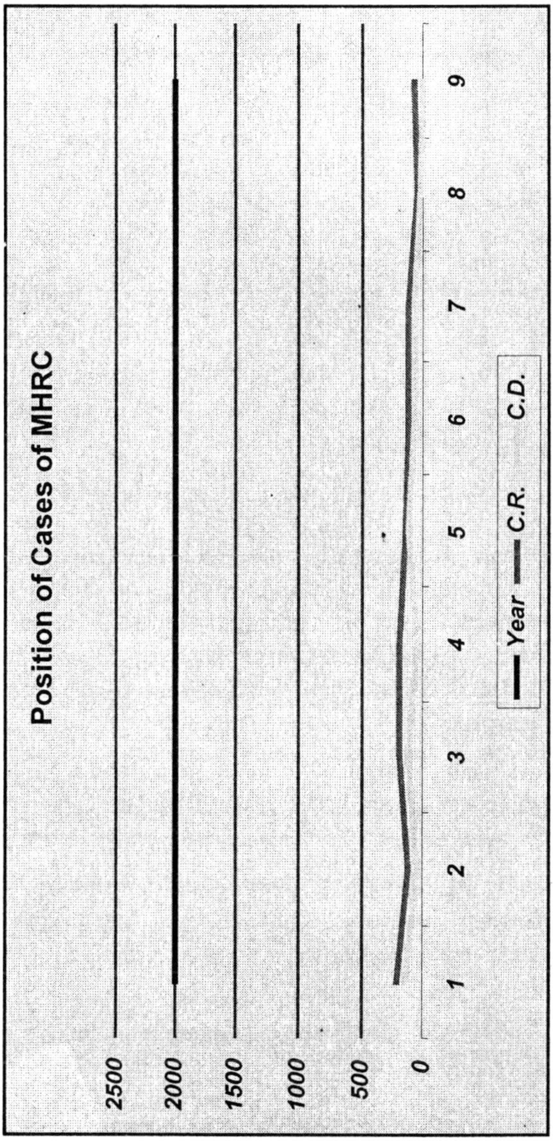

1-1999, 2-2000, 3-2001, 4-2002, 5-2003, 6-2004, 7-2005, 8-2006, 9-2007

C.R- Cases Registered   C.D-Cases Disposed

Case No. 1

Case of hit and run motor accident caused by Army vehicle and adequate Compensation

'A' w/o (L) 'B' of Bamon Leikai, P.S. Mangjil, Imphal East filed a petition to the Commission stating that her husband, 'B' was killed in a motor accident caused by an army vehicle at Tiddim road between Keishampat and Kwakeithal, Imphal on 10/2/2000 but the police could not identify the army vehicle in spite of registering FIR No. 56 (2)2000IPS of Imphal P.S. u/s 279/338/304-A/427 IPC. The complainant stated that she was unable to ascertain to whom her petition should be filed for compensation. In her complaint she prayed for legal action against the Central/State government and its concerned authorities so as to make a scheme for payment of compensation in the case of hit and run motor accident u/s 161,162 and 163of the Motor Vehicles Act, 1988.

Acting upon the case the Commission sought report from the Secretary (Transport), Government of Manipur on whether the official or authorities to whom the application under the scheme for payment of compensation in the case of hit and run motor accidents u/s 163 Of the Motor Vehicle Act,1988 had been specified for Manipur.

The Director of Transport, Manipur furnished a report[30] with a copy of solatium scheme 1989 framed under section 163/91of the Motor Vehicles Act.

After that 'C' on behalf of the petitioner informed the Commission that an application for compensation under the solatium scheme would be filed with the concerned Claims Enquiry Officer.

In view of the above, the Commission considered the case as disposed and closed the file.

Case No. 2

Taking Action for Stopping the Locals bathing, washing etc. in the Historical, Religious, Sacred Place 'Thanga-Pat' at Kangla (MHRC Case No.112 of 2005)

The Secretary of *Maichou Ningshing Lup,* Khurai filed a complaint alleging that because of washing and bathing the historical sacred place known as 'Thanga-Pat' has been badly polluted resulting supply of water from the area became health hazard. It is alleged in the complaint petition that water of that area was supplied to the nearby hotels and other residents. The organization also submitted an application to the Chief Secretary government of Manipur on 16/11/2005 in this regard. The same issue was also raised in 'Ireibak' on 29/8/2005. But the state government had not taken any action in this regard.

The Commission called report/comments from the Chief Secretary Government of Manipur.

The Under Secretary (Art and Culture) Government of Manipur forwarded the comments of the Superintendent of Archeology[31]. The Superintendent furnished the steps taken by the Kangla Fort Board to prevent further pollution of the Kangla Thanga-Pat. These are –

1. Publication of 'Public Notice' to prevent pollution of Kangla Thanga-Pat (Outer Mout) in the local news papers.
2. Notice Boards had been erected in conspicuous places of Kangla Thanga-Pat (Outer Mout).
3. The matter had been reported to S.P. Imphal West, for necessary action against those who violated the instructions of Kangla Fort Board.

The Superintendent also informed that bathing, washing etc at Kangla Thanga-Pat had been effectively checked.

In his reply to the comments of the Superintendent, the Secretary of *Maichou Ningshing Lup* said that in spite of displaying sign boards and letter to S.P. Imphal West still as usual people were taking bath and washing their dirty cloths etc and out of these people not a single one was booked or punished.

On that the administrator of Kangla Fort Board informed the Commission that the department of Archaeology by an order dated 7/9/2006 posted 'A' as attendant at the Outer Moat of Kangla to watch against the bathing, washing of cloths, vehicles etc.

Further the administrator of Kangla Fort Board[32] informed the Commission that the Kangla Fort Board had banned bathing, washing of cloths, vehicles and fetching of water. He also informed that the Board also sought assistance from the S.P. Imphal West and Commanding Officer of 1st I.R.B. Manipur in the regard. Further he informed that the Public Health Engineering Department, Government of Manipur had also cleaned the moat to maintain hygienic condition.

In view of the above, the Commission in its judgment order viewed that positive steps were taken to strictly prohibit bathing and washing etc in the Thanga-Pat and accordingly closed the case.

Case No. 3

Denial of Right to Education by Manipur University (MHRC Case No. 20 of 2000)

'A', a student from Churachandpur filed a complaint stating that he was initially enrolled as a regular student for the T.D.C. Arts course under Manipur University at Churachandpur college. However because of the ethnic disturbances that erupted at Churachandpur forcing the closure of all educational establishments he had sought to pursue his studies by appearing as a private candidate for the second year T.D.C examination in 1997 for the said course. He applied for permission and granted for the same by the authorities of Manipur University which allotted him with the Roll No. 610248 with M.B.College Imphal as the centre wherein he appeared. When the result published he could not find his Roll No. on the list of successful candidates supposing that he could not passed. Accordingly he applied for Mark-Sheet of the said examination to enable him to re-appear.

But inspite of approaching since 1997 Manipur University authorities denied to him the mark-sheet which results denying of his right to further education.

The Commission recommended that the Manipur University had to issue the mark-sheet within two weeks from 10/2/2000 (date of order) and said the Controller of Examination of Manipur University to submit his action taking report to the Commission on or before 26/2/2000.

But the Controller of Examination did not submit the report within due time. Accordingly the Commission issued two reminders, but no response was received. The Commission again issued a reminder dated 14/6/2000 to Dr. 'B', Controller of Examination of Manipur University for his personal attention to the matter and to send the action taken report to the Commission by 1/7/2000.

Deputy Controller of Examination of Manipur University[33] intimated the Commission that he had informed the complainant to collect the mark-sheet on production of registration certificate. He also cited that the delay in providing action taken report was due to heavy work for finalization of T.D.C second year examination, 1999 followed by cease work strike by the staff of the University.

In view of the above the Commission in its order dated 4/7/2000 stated that Manipur University had complied with the recommendation of the Commission and accordingly the case was closed.

Case No. 4

Case for In-action of the Officer In Charge of Lamphel Police Station in discharging his Duties (MHRC Case No. 116 of 2005)

'A' of Thamnapokpi, Moirang Awang Leikai, P.S.Moirang, Bishnupur filed a complaint stating that she loved 'B', S/O 'C' of Thangapat Bamon Leikai, P.O. and P.S. Prompat, Imphal West. 'B' the accused person always insisted her to elope for marriage, and then she decided to elope to enter into a wed-lock. As such she eloped with 'B' on 22/10/2005 saturday at about 2 p.m. from the place of Langol Ningthou and on the same day both of the went to the B's house and spent over night and lived as husband and wife. But on the next day four elderly persons including 'C' father of 'B' went to her house to inform her parents about the elopement and subsequent formality including marriage at a proper date. Since then several dates were fixed for fixing of marriage date and for marriage but no marriage had taken place.

Accordingly on 12/12/2005 she along with her mother and aunty went to the Lamphel Police Station and complained in written to take any action against the accused. But the competent authorities refused to accept the written complaint submitted by her. She stated that the officials' flatly refused to discharge their duties and lot of harassment had been caused to her and no necessary action had been taken so far by the concerned authority. Finally on 15/12/2005 at about 8 p.m. the official accepted the complaint copy after detaining her along with her mother and aunty long hours.

She further stated that it was very unfortunate on the part of the officer in charge of Lamphel Police Station failing to perform his bounden duties. She also stated that the accused person gave a great insult to her which amounts to death in living and humiliation which it amounted to even attempting suicide herself due to loss of respect and prestige in the society.

The Commission called detailed report from the D.G.P. Manipur. The Addl. D.G. of Police (Trg/HR/HG) of Manipur forwarded to the Commission the detailed report submitted by S.P. Imphal West.[34]

The report stated that no police case was registered as the incident was purely of the civil nature and no cognizable offence which in police had no power to investigate. Accordingly the complainant had been directed to go to competent court as per provision of section 155(i) Cr.P.C. However, the complaint report was entered vide General Diry Entry No. 529/LPS/2005 dated 15/12/2005 of Lamphel P.S. The report also stated that there was no ground or reason to make any sort of harassment or any unnecessary gesture to the complainant on the part of the police.

In her reply to the above mentioned report the complainant disagreed with police report and stated that the nature of the offence not to co-operate in fixing up a marriage date so committed by the accused was clear intention of insulting the modesty of a woman. Section 509 of IPC makes intention to insult the modesty of a woman the essential ingredient of the offence.

The Commission sought statements from the accused and O/C Lamphel P.S. But they remained absent on proceedings date of 13/10/2006. On proceeding date 8/12/2006 the complainant was absent. The Commission accepted the report of the S.P. Imphal West and accordingly closed the case.

Case No. 5

Claiming of Insurance Money from LICI (MHRC Case No. 6 of 2005)

'A' W/O Late 'B', Ex-Inspector of Police, Khurai Thangjam Leikai, Imphal in her complaint stated that her husband was serving as officer-in-charge of police station at Kakching and he was shot dead by some unidentified armed youths, at Kakching Phousupat, near Kakching Higher Secondary School, on 17/11/2000, while he was doing his duty as officer-in-charge of police station, Kakching. During his life time her husband draw the Death Claim Policy No. 490199314, of the Life Insurance Corporation of India. After his death she as nominee made many request in written for releasing the available amount under the said policy. Inspite of releasing the amount the Manager LICI, Imphal Branch, asked her to produce final report of the police in connection with F.I.R No. 113(11) 2000, Kakching P.S. She further stated that the S.P. Thoubal District did not give final police report either to her or to the Manager LICI, Imphal Branch.

Acting upon the case, the Commission called report from the Manager LICI, Imphal Branch, Khoyathong National Highway, Imphal, Superintendent of Police, Thoubal District and officer-in-charge of Kakching Police Station, Thoubal.

Manager LICI in his reply said that he had sent all the papers relating to the death claim under the policy no. 490199314 to the

LICI, Silchar Divisional Office, Silchar, Assam which had been admitted by the Divisional Office vide its fax message dated 31/1/2005. He also hoped that he will send the discharge voucher as early as possible for payment of the claim immediately on receipt of the other claim papers from the Divisional Office at Silchar.

The S.P. Thoubal sent a detailed report[35] on the case. In the report it was shown that Inspector 'B' the officer-in-charge of Kakching Police Station was shot to death through bullet injury by unknown U.Gs[36] during an encounter between police commandos and unknown U.Gs while returning from RIMS Morgue to Kakching P.S.with other police personals in the official Gypsy at about 5.50 p.m. on 17/11/2000.

On 17/3/2005 the LICI informed the Commission that the Manager LICI, Imphal Branch, had submitted a discharge voucher of net amount payable to the complainant to the tune of Rs. 1 lakh and the nominee can sign on the revenue stamp and on presentation to the local office the money could be released to her.

In the final order the Commission agreed with the LICI, Imphal Branch that as the money had been received by the complainant, no further inquiry is needed and accordingly closed the case.

Case No. 6

Case against Kakching Police Station for not taking Necessary Action (MHRC Case No. 40 of 2004)

'A', D/O 'B' of Hiyaglam Makha Leikai, P.O and P.S. Kakching, Thoubal District filed a complaint stating that on 3/4/2004 at about 10 p.m. while she was sleeping on her bed, 'C' S/O (L) 'D' of Hiyanglam Mayai Leikai, who had been taking shelter at her house raped her. After committing the crime he threatened her of dire consequences if she disclosed the matter to anybody. Again on 7/4/2004 the accused person raped her on her bed. She also stated that she could not disclose the matter to her father. Subsequently she became pregnant and reported the matter to the accused person. In that the accused person suggested to have abortion under threat and accordingly on 23/5/2004 he had taken her to one Dr. 'E' of Langmeidong and conducted abortion without her consent.

She also stated that she lodged a written report to the officer-in-charge Kakching Police Station FIR No.28 (5)2004 Kakching P.S. u/s 376/313 IPC and 25(1-C) Arms Act. She alleged that the concerned investigation officer of the case did not make any attempt to arrest the culprit till date. And instead of arresting the culprit by performing their bounded duty the police personnel of Kakching Police Station demanded money from her family. Due to the inaction of the police, the culprit had been threatening her and her family members to withdraw the report lodged at the police station.

The Commission called report from the DGP, Manipur. Addl. DGP (HR), Manipur forwarded the detailed report of S.P. Thoubal[37] to the Commission. In the report the S.P. stated that during investigation 5 witnesses were examined and the accused was arrested and sent to police custody for 7 days and after that accused got bail from the court.

The S.P. in the report mentioned that although the victim said that she was raped but the accused said that the intercourse was with consent as they loved each other. Further the S.P. stated that according to the verdict of the victim the accused had been taking shelter at victim's home since 24/3/2004 and on 3/4/2004 she was raped even her father was also there in the room. The report also stated that Dr. 'E' during examination said that the abortion was done on the consent of both the parties.

The Addl. DGP (HR), Manipur again forwarded a letter of the S.P. Thoubal District[38] to the Commission which informed that as per the expert opinion the case wouldn't stand in the court in the midst of meager evidence and for this the investigation of the case had been closed and returned in Final Report.

In view of the above the Commission viewed that there was hardly anything to be done then by the Commission and accordingly closed the case.

Case No. 7

Taking Away of 15 Minor Children by American Couple (MHRC Case No.7 of 2001)

'A' Ex MLA filed a complaint dated 19/1/2001to the Commission stating that 15 tribal orphan / destitute girl children of 3 to 7 years had been taken away by a couple Mr. and Mrs. 'B' through one 'C' from Manipur to Bangalore with promise of giving them good education. But it turned out that they were not given any sort of education, proper food and they were kept isolated far away from the society and since the purpose of their sending them there was not served their guardians wished to take them back to Manipur but that also had been resisted by the couple and the guardians were not able to get back those poor little girl children and the concerned state authority had not taken up any positive action in the matter.

The Commission called for a detailed report on the matter from the Commissioner/Secretary, Social Welfare government of Manipur and from the Director of Social Welfare, Government of Manipur. Accordingly the Commissioner submitted a detailed report[39] to the Commission.

In the report the Commissioner informed that on 13/12/2000 the Commissioner (Social Welfare) office of Manipur received a letter dated 8/12/2000 from the Director of Women and Child Development, Government of Karnataka stating that an organization called Harvest Workers Trust run by an American Couple had illegally confined 20 children at their premises and of these children 15 were from Manipur and the organization was not a registered one. Accordingly children were removed from there and admitted to government observation home for their safety.

Accordingly arrangements were made for shifting the children to Manipur and two officials from Manipur reached Bangalore on 19/12/2000 to bring the children and 24/12/2000 was fixed as a date for bringing the children from Bangalore to Calcutta and the children would reach 25/12/2000 in Imphal. But as 'B' the American who owned the Harvest Workers Trust filed a case to the High Court of Karnataka, the process of shifting got delayed.

Ultimately because of the favourable judgment of High Court of Karnataka children were brought to Imphal escorted by personnel of Manipur and Karnataka government and on the basis of the decision of the Juvenile Justice Board dated 9/2/2001 the children were handed over to their respective guardians.

The Commission further asked the Commissioner (Social Welfare) Government of Manipur to submit names and particulars of the father, mother and also the names and particulars of the persons to whom the children had been handed over and their relationship with the children. Accordingly the Commissioner of Social Welfare, Government of Manipur submitted report[40] to the Commission.

In view of the above report the Commission closed the case.

Case No. 8

Payment of Ex-Gratia on the Death of Wife (MHRC Case No. 45 of 2004)

'A' of Terakhongshangbi Leimram Leikai, P.S. Moirang, Bishnupur filed a complaint stating that his wife namely late 'B' was kidnapped/abducted by some unknown armed personals suspected to be extremists on 29/5/2003 at about 8 P.M. near house. She was also physically assaulted by the abductors with deadly weapons and died at the district hospital, Churachandpur on 30/5/2003 at about 5.30 A.M. before receiving medical treatment.

Accordingly he filed a petition to the Deputy Commissioner Bishnupur on 23/7/2003 praying for award of ex-gratia grant for the death/murder of his wife. The report in connection with the award of ex-gratia grant was submitted to the Deputy Commissioner Bishnupur by the S.D.O Moirang on the basis of the report of Sub-Deputy Collector of Moirang. But the steps/ actions for award of ex-gratia in respect of the death of 'B' were not taken up by the concerned departments without any reason.

The Commission called report from DGP Manipur and Spl. Secretary (Home) Government of Manipur. Accordingly Joint Secretary (Home) government of Manipur[41] and Addl. DGP (HR), Manipur[42] submitted report to the Commission on the basis of examination of witnesses.

According to the report on 29/5/2003 the members of Women Welfare Association/*Meira Paibi* of Terakhongshangbi had called a meeting in which four persons including the deceased were summoned at the office of the association for giving warning to them for their alleged immoral acts. But the meeting was postponed at about 3.30 p.m. due to their inability to arrive at any decision. By that time six to seven unknown persons suspected to be members of U.G. organization in civil dress appeared before the association office and took away the four persons including the deceased to an open place and tortured them by beating. Before leaving the place, these persons told *Meira Paibis* that as the *Meira Paibis* could not arrive at any conclusion these four persons were taken by them to inflict punishment on them for their loose character.

The report also stated that after a thorough investigation it came to the knowledge of the police that the crime was committed by armed miscreants suspected to be members of banned organization namely United National Liberation Front.

From the above report it was clear that the crime was committed by the armed miscreants. The Commission in its judgment order directed the Chief Secretary, Government of Manipur to pay the ex-gratia to the complainant as admissible under the law as early as possible.

Case No. 9

Arrest without Arrest Memo (MHRC Case No. 66 of 2003)

'A' W/O 'B', P.S. Wangoi, Imphal West filed a complaint to the Commission stating that in the midnight of 21/05/2003 some unknown security personnel in uniform intruded into her residential house at Samurou Makha Leikai and pulled out her sons 'C' and 'D' and also 'E' (C's Uncle) and 'F' (E's Son) for unknown reason and tortured all of them severely by beating with sticks and by kicking continually for the whole night and next morning, and then took away 'C' who was too weak even to stand up due to torture without issuing any arrest memo. And since then his whereabouts could not be located even after the petitioner and his family members had made query to the police station and they were informed that the arrestee had not been handed over to the civil police. She further stated that under the circumstances she and her family members were much worried about the life and personal safety of her young child.

The Commission called report from the DGP Manipur to be submitted within 24 hours. The DGP forwarded the report of Sr.S.P. Imphal West[43] (Letter of Sr.S.P. Imphal West to DGP Manipur) to the Commission. The report said that the arrestee, 'C', 15 years old, had not been handed over to the police station and the Commander 9 Sector C/O 99 APO had been requested to intimate the whereabouts of the said individual.

The Commission asked the DGP, Manipur to file further report immediately within 24 hours. The Commission took serious note of the case and every day the proceedings of the case had been done. The DGP, Manipur on 30/5/2003 informed the Commission that 'C' had been handed over to O.C. Lilong P.S.

The Commission further sought report about arrest memo from DGP, Manipur. The DGP, Manipur filed a report with enclosing the letter of the S.P. Thoubal District which said that on 26/5/2003 at 10.35 p.m. complainant Hav. 'G' No. 172858 of 17 AR lodged a written report with the O.C. Lilong P.S. against accused 'C' which was registered as FIR No. 17(5)2003 LIL PS U/S 121/121-A/212 IPC and 10/13 UA(P) Act and the accused was produced before the Magistrate. The report was accompanied with a copy of arrest memo showing date and time of arrest as 26/5/2003 at 0240 hrs.

In view of the above the Commission closed the proceedings of the case.

Case No. 10

Case of Abduction and Rape (MHRC Case No. 31 of 2004)

One report had been received by the Commission from S.P. Thoubal stating that on 16/5/2004 at 5 p.m. 'A' (27) W/O 'B' of Athokpam Makha Laiharaobam Maya reported that on 3/5/2004 at about 8 a.m. she was abducted by cheating from Khangabok Makha Leikai to Moreh Bazar and on the same day at about 7.30 p.m. she was raped by 'C' (47) S/O (L) 'D' of Athokpam Makha Laiharaobam Maya. In that report she also mentioned that two other associates namely 'E' and 'F' of Khangabok Mayai Leikai were also involved in her abduction. A case under FIR No. 59(5)04 TBL PS u/s 365/120-B/376 IPC was registered at TBL PS and was investigated into.

The Commission sought report from the DGP, Manipur. The DGP, Manipur forwarded the reports of S.P.Thoubal to the Commission. According to those reports during investigation witnesses were examined, accused person was arrested and remanded into police custody by order of CJM/Thoubal.

The final report showed that according to the medical examination report of both victim and main accused person there was no evidence to show whether the accused had committed the sexual offence. Further the report showed that there were no marks of struggle/ violence on the body of the victim. And in due course of investigation the case was closed and returned in Final Report under FR No. 108/04/TBL PS date 14/9/04 for insufficiency of evidence[44]. In view of the above report the Commission closed the case.

Case No. 11

Case on Right to Education (MHRC Case No. 4 of 2006)

The Chairman Lamlaba Village Authority filed a complaint to the Commission stating that Lamlaba Junior High School was the only educational institution in Lamlaba Circle covering about 15 villages of Tamei Sub-Division in the Tameng-long District of Manipur. He stated that only one undergraduate teacher was posted in the school and because of it number of students dropped out of school. This had put their academic career as well as their future in jeopardy. The village Chairman drew the attention of MHRC as this was a matter of violation of fundamental rights to education.

Taking serious view of the case, the Commission sent notice to the Director of Education (Schools), Manipur to fulfil the need. As a result two primary teachers were reverted back to the Lamlaba Junior High School from their engagement at SSA, Tamenglong. The School got three teaching staff including one Head Master in-charge.

Other Activities of the SHRCs

Visits of Jails, Police Stations

According to Article 12(C) of the Protection of Human Rights Act 1993, the state Commission is empowered to visit under intimation to the state government, any jail or any other institution under the control of the state government, where persons are detained or lodged for purpose of treatment, reformation or protection. The purpose of visit is to study the living conditions of the inmates and make necessary recommendations.

Assam Human Rights Commission[45]

Members of the AHRC visited different jails, police stations throughout the state. Shri Justice S.N.Bhargava, the then Chairperson and Shri Justice T.C.Das, the then Member of AHRC in the last week of May, 1996 visited the District Jail at Guwahati. On the basis of the visit the then Chairperson Shri Justice S.N. Bhargava made several recommendations to the Chief Minister of Assam as mentioned below

Recommendations of AHRC

i) As the Jail is more than century old and situated in a thickly place, the Commission recommended for shifting of Guwahati Jail to a place outside the city.

ii) Land of the jail may be disposed off by public auction and the money raised may be spent on the construction of the new jail with all the modern facilities at a new site.

iii) On the basis of complaint made by the jail inmates the Commission recommended for taking measures in order to improve the hygienic condition in jail, supply of medicines to prisoners and essential repairs of the staff quarters.

The Commission members also visited several jails in different districts, such as Cachar (Shri Justice S.N.Bhargava, Chairperson, 1996), Karimganj (Shri Justice S.N.Bhargava, Chairperson, 1996), Lakhimpur (Shri Justice T.C.Das, Member, 1996), Tezpur (Shri Justice S.N.Bhargava, Chairperson, 1999), Dhubri (A. Mazid, Member, 2003) and made necessary recommendations.

On 27/2/2003 A.Mazid the then Member visited District Jail at Goalpara. Women inmates complained that there was leackage of rain water from the roof of their ward causing inconvenience. Moreover sanitary latrine system in some place of the ward was worn out emitting foul smell. Accordingly the commission member gave necessary instruction for taking action. The jails were not found to be over crowded.

A. Mazid, the then member, AHRC, also visited police station of Dhubri town accompanied by the S.P. to oversee whether all 11 requirements for prevention of custodial violence as contained in D.K.Basu's case (1997(1)SCC 416) had been complied with by the police officers. The Member found that the police station complied with all the requirements except very important requirement, i.e. No.6- regarding entry in the diary about arrest of person and disclosure of the name of the next friend of the detainee who had been informed about the arrest and the name and address of the police official in whose custody the arrestee was. Accordingly the Member in presence of the S.P. instructed the police officer to comply with requirement No.6 in toto.

Manipur Human Rights Commission[46]

In the initial year of the establishment, MHRC Members visited two Central Jails of Manipur. On 22/1/99 the Commission Members visited the Imphal Central Jail and on 23/1/99 the members visited Sajiwa Central Jail and recommended certain improvements to the state government. After 1999 the Commission did not visit any of the jails till January, 2008. It is saddening to note that it never visited the jails located outside Imphal, the capital town.

Visits of Custodial Homes / Hospitals / Relief Camps etc:

Assam Human Rights Commission:[47]

In the year 1996 Shri Justice S.N.Bhargava, the then Chaiperson and Shri P.Kalita the then member made visits to certain institutions under the Department of Social Welfare, Government of Assam. Some of which are-

i) State Home for Women, Guwahati,

ii) Vagrant Home, Guwahati,

iii) Observation Home, Guwahati,

iv) Training-cum-Production Centre, Guwahati

v) Observation-cum-Special Home for Juvenile Girls, Guwahati,

vi) Home for Destitute Women and Helpless Widows, Guwahati,

vii) Kamala Nehru T.B. Hospital, Nagaon,

vii) Bal Bhavan Orphanage of Shankar Mission, Nagaon,

vii) Civil Hospital, Nagaon and Civil Hospital, Mangaldai,

The then Chairperson Shri Justice S.N. Bhargava with a member of Assam State Commission for Women visited Central Destitute Home, Silchar.

On March, 2003 Dr. H.N. Kalita member, AHRC visited Observation centre of Jorhat and recommended certain remedial measures. On 5/4/04 the Commission members made surprise visit to Jorhat Civil Hospital for inspection. The Commission found that the patients were well attended and sanitary system was satisfactory.

Shri Justice S.N.Bhargava, Chairperson, Shri P.Kalita, member and Shri A.K. Choudhury, Secretary of AHRC visited some relief camps of Kokrajhar and Bongaigaon Districts. These relief camps were set up for the victims of ethnic violence that occurred in 1996. The main problem of these camps was of medical and health facilities.

The Commission was apprised of the invaluable services rendered by different non-governmental organizations. The commission held discussion with officials and non-officials about various problems faced by them. The possible solutions were also discussed. The Commission recommended necessary steps in this regard to the state government.

Manipur Human Rights Commission[48]

In 1999 the Commission visited the Regional Institute of Medical Sciences (RIMS) at Lamphelpat and the J.N.Hospital at porompat. During visit at RIMS the Commission Members talked with two sisters who were earlier subjected to torture by CRPF and made necessary recommendations.

On 24/1/99 the Commission members visited Shri B.B.Paul Mental Development Home for mentally retarded children at Mongsangei and requested the government for purchasing file covers etc manufactured by this Home.

On 23/1/99 the Commission visited the Government Blind School and Deaf and Dumb School at Takyelpat and made discussion with the staff and students regarding their problems.

On 23/3/99 the then Chairperson Shri Justice S.N.Bhargava, the member Sarvasri L.Rabindra Singh, Yambem Laba, Kh. Chonjohn of MHRC visited the Thanga Island in Loktak lake and met a large number of residents. Shri Kh. Bidhu Singh, President of the Joint Action Committee presented a memorandum listing excesses of the army during operation Loktak. Most of the victims narrated their ordeals to the visiting MHRC members. The Chairperson MHRC forwarded the Memorandum to the National Human Rights Commission along with recommendation for immediate relief and rehabilitation of the victims.

Spreading of Human Rights Awareness

According to section 12(h) of the Protection of the Human Rights Act 1993 the state commission has the responsibility to spread human rights literacy among various section of society and promote awareness of the safeguards available for the protection of these rights through publications, the media, seminars and other available means. Creating human rights culture necessitates spreading of awareness. "Human rights play a very important part as fifty percent of the population is illiterate and where the concept of human rights is yet to be understood."[49]

In order to spread awareness both AHRC and MHRC have taken several steps such as conducting training programmes, workshops, orientation programmes, seminar, discussions, etc.

Assam Human Rights Commission[50]

From February 6 to February 8 1997 the AHRC conducted a NHRC sponsored seminar on human rights and highlighted on such issues like human rights- moral and ethical values, human rights- woman and child, human rights education and awareness, role of NGO and media etc. The objective of the seminar was to spread awareness about rights and devise means to protect these. The then Chairperson, AHRC referred in detail about the jurisdiction and functions of AHRC. The seminar was attended by jurists, politicians, advocates, educationists, administrative officials, NGO activists, etc.

Over the years the AHRC has organized a number of seminars with objective of spreading awareness among different sections of people about rights. These are attended predominantly by students, educationists, and common people. Basically these seminars are organized by several institutions and helped by AHRC so as to reach common people more effectively with the help of NGOs although the AHRC itself also organizes some seminars.

In the sphere of violation of human rights of the people in North East India, the role of police and army personnel is no less important. So, it is necessary to spread awareness among them. For this training programmes and discussions were arranged by the Commission at different points of time.

Training programme on human rights for Deputy S.P. Trainees 39th Batch was held at Assam Police Training College, Dergaon from 31/5/04 to 4/6/04. On 21/6/03 one member of the Commission met higher authorities of Assam Police Training College at Dergaon to stress on the need for human rights education amongst the police personnel.

Table 3.5: Some of the Seminars for Spreading Human Rights Awareness (In collaboration with AHRC)

Sl. No.	*Date*	*Title of Seminar*	*Host Institution/Venue*
1.	11/12/96	Human Rights	Dept. of Law, Guwahati University
2.	06-08/02/97	Human Rights	Rabidra Bhawan, Guwahati.
3.	June, 1999	Right to Participation of Child	
4.	30/09/2000	Human Rights	Bishnu Nirmala Bhawan, Guwahati, Organised by Institute of Peace, Disarmament and Environment Protection, Nagpur and Citizens' Collective.
5.	14/10/2000	Human Rights	Nagaon Law College, Nagaon.
6.	10/12/03	Human Values: Armed Forces and the State	Youth Leadership Centre, Dibrugarh
7.	21/2/04	Human Rights	Human Rights Awareness and Protection Forum, Guwahati.
8.	07/04/04	Human rights and Human Values	Youth Leadership Centre, Dibrugarh.
9.	28-29/11/04	Human Rights	Guwahati
10.	28-29/11/06	Human rights	Assam administrative Staff College, Guwahati.

Source: Office of the Assam Human Rights Commission, Guwahati

Table 3.6

Orientation Programmes Conducted for Spreading Human Rights Awareness

Sl. No.	*Date*	*Title of Orientation Programme*	*Host Institution/Venue*
1.	15/07/98	Camp on Health and Neutration	
2.	08/06/99	Programme for Media Personals	Administrative Staff College, Guwahati
3.	22/01/2000	Rights of Children	Oakland English School, Guwahati
4.	02/02/2000	Rights of Children	Ramdia Higher Secondary School, Hajo
5.	12/08/2000	Course for Northeast Frontier Railway Officials	AHRC Complex

Source: Office of the Assam Human Rights Commission

The Commission members also attended a number of discussions on human rights. Some of these are 'Women's Human Rights-Past and Present-Empowerment of Women' organized by Assam State Commission for Women (1999), informal discussion of AHRC members with magistrates, police personnel, administrative officers, etc. were arranged by Deputy Commissioner, Dhubri on 1/3/03 to exchange views on human rights and the Protection of Human Rights Act 1993.

The Commission also conducts orientation programmes for spreading awareness.

The Commission also organized District level awareness programme on rights of child (24/9/98), North Eastern Regional Public Hearing on Right to Health Care at Guwahati (28/11/2004), training course for law students of Guwahati University law college (27/4/2000), and J.B.Law college (13/5/2000) particularly on rights of women, children and disabled etc.

Besides these the Commission Members attended several discussions, meetings, delivered lectures, delivered key note addresses in seminars in several times.

Media is the most important communicating means in today's world. Considering this the Commission used media for spreading awareness.

Press conference on human rights and the different aspects of the activities of AHRC held at Guwahati on 23/9/96 was attended by Chairperson and Members and on 17/12/96 at Silchar was attended by Chairperson only.

A talk on child labour was telecasted from Guwahati *Doordarshan* which was attended by Shri Paramananda Kalita on 22/4/99 to show the child labour scenario in North east India. Shri P. Kalita also attended a panel discussion in Assamese broadcast by Guwahati station of All India Radio (AIR) on Human Rights Movements for women, a talk on Twenty First century and Universal Declaration of Human Rights was broadcasted by Guwahati AIR on 26/12/99.

For the purpose of disseminating information about human rights, the members of the Commission not only attended and participated in discussions they had taken important step toward spreading the knowledge of human rights to the different segments of government employees. Mr. Justice S.N.Bhargava, the then Chairperson AHRC wrote to the Chief Minister of Assam vide letter No. AHRC (CMA) 97/253 dated 13/5/99 requesting him to issue instruction to all government departments to allot some time in order to introduce the subject of human rights to the participants. The state Government issued circular No. CMS 94/ 96/188 dated 25/5/99 directing all the commissioners and secretaries for introducing the concept of human rights accordingly.

Mr. Justice S.N. Bhargava, the then Chairperson, AHRC recommended to the state government on 5/4/99 for naming a road as '*Manab Adhikar Path* (Human Rights Road)' in greater Guwahati in order to raise awareness of rights among the public.

The AHRC also published Newsletters. For the purpose of spreading awareness it has published one book, few leaflets in English and Assamese.

Manipur Human Rights Commission[51]

In order to spread awareness among people the Manipur Human Rights Commission embarked on a series of Human Rights Awareness Campaign throughout the state in the year 2005. The Commission has planned to conduct campaigns in district head quarters first and then in sub-divisions of the districts and from there on the remote villages. The first leg of the series was launched on 26/11/2005 in the Churachandpur district head quarter. In the second phase on 18/11/2006 at Youth Hostel, Ukhrul District and on 10/1/2007 at Moreh, Chandel District the campaigns held. The campaigns were participated by local club members, NGO personnel, administrative officials, common public and others.

The Commission also organized seminar on 'Rights of Indigenous People' at state guest house on 9/8/2006 attended by NGO personnel, officials and others, on 1/5/2006 seminar on 'Rights of Labours' at the state guest house was attended by Labour officials, educationists, judges, labourers and others. The Commission also organized workshop on Human Rights education at the state guest house on 10/12/05 which was attended by academicians. From this workshop it is recommended that human rights education should be included in University curriculum.

In the afternoon of 31/3/99 the Commission members met the members of the Bar and Bench at the District Court premises. In that gathering the concept of human rights and jurisdiction of the Human Rights Commissions were highlighted. The Commission Members also discussed in detail with the judicial officers about the inspections of jails.

Besides these the Commission members also attended seminars, meetings, discussions as they called and discussed about the different aspects of human rights. The state Commission also published two News Letters, one leaflet in order to spread awareness.

Appeal made to the State Governments

Assam Human Rights Commission[52]

Mr. Justice S.N.Bhargava, Chairperson AHRC[53] urged the Chief Minister to release the prisoners crossing the age of 70 years on probation under the supervision of District Probation Officer. Justice S.N.Bhargava[54] suggested the Chief Minister for enacting law prohibiting throwing and disposal of non-biodegradable garbage like plastic bags in drains, roads etc.

He wrote a letter to the Chief Minister of Assam[55]requesting the construction of flyovers at Ulubari and Ganeshguri with the help of some foreign agencies so that the traffic jams occurring regularly at these places could be solved.[56]

Manipur Human Rights Commission[57]

On 30/3/99 the Commission Members met the Chief Minister, Law Minister, Chief Secretary, Government of Manipur in the office chamber of the Chief Minister and explained to them the difficulties faced by the Commission. Subsequently, the Chairperson sent a letter addressed to the Chief Minister in this regard.

Research Done by the State Commissions

According to section 12(g) of the Protection of Human Rights Act 1993, it is one of the responsibilities of the state commission to undertake and promote research.

Between 1998 and 1999 the Assam Human Rights Commission completed the following two UNICEF projects.

i) Child Labour in Guwahati City.

ii) Situational Analysis of Girl Child in Assam.

In the project it is recommended that local laws relating to children needed to be amended. After this no research projects have been undertaken by the Commission.

No research study has been undertaken by the Manipur Human Rights Commission till date.

Effectiveness

In order to understand the role of the SHRCs fully it is essential to understand the effectiveness. Effectiveness can be understood through the discussion of following points-

i) Continuity: The Commissions are in existence in both states for more than a decade. Since their establishment a number of cases have been registered and disposed by them although the numbers are decreasing in recent times. They are able to undertake other functions as specified in the Act. The receipt and expenditure pattern of the Commission indicates the survival and continuity of the Commissions.

ii) Independence: Independence is a very relative term. An independent institution is one which is free from political pressures and several other factors that may affect its work. Although apparently both AHRC and MHRC are independent but both of them has certain links and limits with the state governments of Assam and Manipur respectively like the financial matters.

iii) Resource: Section 33 subsection 1 of the Protection of Human Rights Act 1993 lays down that the state government shall, after due appropriation made by Legislature by law in this behalf, pay to the State Commission by way of grants such sums

Table 3.7

Information Relating to Budget of Assam Human Rights Commission

Financial Year	*Amount proposed*	*Amount sanctioned*	*Amount Released*	*Amount Not Released*
1996-1997	-	-	Rs. 22.09 *Lakhs*	-
1997-1998	-	-	Rs.19.99 *Lakhs*	-
1998-1999	-	-	Rs.29.07 *Lakhs*	-
1999-2000	Rs.1,50,3800.00 *Lakhs*	Rs.30.00 *Lakhs*	Rs.19.99 *Lakhs*	Rs.10.01 *Lakhs*
2000-2001	Rs.66,32,179.00 *Lakhs*	Rs.27.00 *Lakhs*	Rs.19.00 *Lakhs*	Rs.8.00 *Lakhs*
2001-2002	Rs.73,87,454.00 *Lakhs*	Rs.27.00 *Lakhs*	Rs.14.00 *Lakhs*	Rs.13.00 *Lakhs*
2002-2003	Rs.89,94,872.00 *Lakhs*	Rs.25.00 *Lakhs*	Rs.23.00 *Lakhs*	Rs.2.00 *Lakhs*
2003-2004	Rs.98,50,599.00 *Lakhs*	Rs.25.00 *Lakhs*	Rs.25.00 *Lakhs*	
2004-2005	Rs.79,17,502.00 *Lakhs*	Rs.27.00 *Lakhs*	Rs.25.84 *Lakhs*	Rs.1.16 *Lakhs*
2005-2006	Rs.78,07,228.00 *Lakhs*	Rs.27.00 *Lakhs*	Rs.25.00 *Lakhs*	Rs.2.00 *Lakhs*
2006-2007	Rs.57,31,364.00 *Lakhs*	Rs.28.00 *Lakhs*	Rs.19.00 *Lakhs*	Rs.9.00 *Lakhs*

Source: Office of the Assam Human Rights Commission

of money as the state government may think fit for being utilized for the purposes of the act.

Subsection 2 of the said Act lays down that the State Commission may spent such sums as it thinks fit for performing the functions under Chapter V of the Act.

Table 3.8

Information Relating to Budget of Manipur Human Rights Commission

Year	*Amount proposed*	*Amount Released*
1999-2000	12.82 *Lakhs*	12.82 *Lakhs*
2000-2001	Not Available	Not Available
2001-2002	14.00 *Lakhs*	14.00 *Lakhs*
2002-2003	Not Available	Not Available
2003-2004	28.68 *Lakhs*	28.68 *Lakhs*
2004-2005	30.00 *Lakhs*	30.00 *Lakhs*
2005-2006	20.00 *Lakhs*	20.00 *Lakhs*
2006-2007	15.00 *Lakhs*	15.00 *Lakhs*
2007-2008	16.00 *Lakhs*	16.00 *Lakhs*

Source: Office of the Manipur Human Rights Commission

From these facts, it is clear that in case of AHRC there is lack of fund. The government is releasing less than 50% of the proposed amount whereas in case of MHRC the government is releasing according to proposed amount.

Section 35 of the Protection of Human Rights Act 1993 provides that the Commission should maintain proper accounts and other records and the accounts should be audited by Comptroller and Auditor General or any other person appointed by him.

According to state Commissions they (state Commissions) maintain proper accounts and records. But till date no audit of the accounts has been done in case of both the commissions.

iv) Operational Efficiency: Efficiency is the basic requirement of any institution. In all activities like its procedure, development of working methods and rules, implementations of such rules etc require efficiency and this depends on the efficiency of staff.

Presently in AHRC there are altogether 15 supporting employees and in MHRC 14 supporting employees though on deputation, performing different tasks.

v) Accessibility: As the State Commissions protect the interests of the public they should be accessible, in order to become effective. For this they have to maintain contacts with relevant departments and institutions. But the Assam Human Rights Commission and the Manipur Human rights Commission maintain contacts with governmental departments and NGOs as per necessity. Till date both the Commissions have not received any foreign delegate though members of both the Commissions attended several national and state level meetings.

In this era of electronics one can easily access the Assam Human Rights Commission through their website www.ahrc.gov.in from any corner of the world. Although the Manipur Human Rights Commission does not have website but one can easily file complaint through email to mhrc@man.nic.in.

vi) Accountability: According to the provisions of the Protection of Human Rights Act 1993 the state commissions are legally and financially accountable to the respective state governments. The state commissions are required to submit report on their activities including the financial report to the respective state governments which will place it before Legislature. These reports are open to all the members for scrutiny and comments.

The AHRC so far has placed two reports to the Assam Government i.e. annual report of 1996-97 and annual reports from 1997-2002. But the Government so far has placed before Legislature only one report i.e. annual report of 1996-97 and was accordingly passed by the Assembly. Till date the MHRC has not submitted any annual report to the state government.

The state commissions' accountability towards public can be shown in different ways. Any person can look the official reports of the commission any time by obtaining formal permission.

Publications are also another means through which Commissions' accountability towards public is understood. Towards this end both AHRC and MHRC publishes newsletters.

Under the provisions of The Protection of Human Rights Act 1993 SHRCs were established with high hopes. But the role of SHRCs of North East India where the human rights condition is critical does not inspire much hope. The facts clearly indicates that since the establishment AHRC did not perform two above said functions and MHRC did not perform three above said functions enlisted in the Act itself. Both the Commissions are lacking in financial matters which is the backbone of any institution. Submission of annual reports is also one of the important functions of the SHRCs as this reflects their working and accountability. Unfortunately, both the Commissions are lagging behind in this respect also.

NOTES & REFERENCES

1. Year of establishment
2. Memo No.1746 dated 15th May, 2003
3. Vide letter No.CR/IX-91/2003/6175 dated 23.7.2003, Memo No.CR/IX-91/04/8707 dated 20.11.2004 and Memo No. CR/IX-91/AHRC/05/852 dated 20.1.2005.
4. By letter No.PRI.135/2005/9 dated 3rd June, 2006
5. Memo No. NM.5/98/415 dated 12.5.2006
6. Memo No.ESSTT/JT.DHS(K)/AHRC/05-06/4248
7. Memo No.HSE/AHRC/23/2005/2547 dated 15.3.2005
8. Memo No.HSE/AHRC/51/2005/8285 dated 8.7.2005
9. No.Esstt/05/4819 dated 30.06.2005
10. Memo No. DMJ.29/2004/36 dated 24th Sept' 2004
11. No. RB/5901 dated 2nd Sept' 2004
12. Memo No .DCL 25/2004/22 dated 18th Sept, 2004
13. Letter No.DN-57/2004/50 dated 14th August, 2004
14. No. PLA.588/2004/7 dated 18th Sept, 2004
15. Memo No.JDHS/DMJ/HRC/06/8681 dated 22nd August, 2006

16. Memo No. KMJ-51/2004/11 dated 27th September, 2004
17. Memo No.C/HRC/07/05/13 dated 20th April, 2005
18. No. IV-26/205/E/2067 dated 13.4.2005
19. Letter No.C.HRC/88/04/42 dated 11th July, 2005
20. No.C/HRC/88/04/40 dated 1.2. 2005
21. Memo No. PNB/CB/88/PT-II/04/702 dated 18th December, 2004
22. Memo No.V/IV-116/05/401 dated 10.1.2005
23. Memo No. 2005/AMC/6113 dated 18.4.2005
24. Memo No ASACS/2005/770 dated 28.4.2005
25. Memo No.SVMJ/AHRC/ME/13/06/19 dated 12th April, 2006.
26. Memo No.KMJ-9/PT-II/2006/127 dated 12th October, 2006
27. Memo NO.MGR/IV/06/AHRC/8650 dated 19-9-2006
28. MDC/IS/(Steno) /06/EA/830 dated 17-8-2006
29. Year of establishment
30. Letter No.1/8/MV/82-II/1082 dated 31/1/2001
31. Letter No. 5/30/2005-S(AC)
32. Letter No. 1/1/05 (Estt./KFB) dated 30/1/2007
33. Letter No.Mu/9/2-13(ii)/99/3156 dated 31 May 2000
34. Letter No. 6/20/SP-IW/05(pt-45/365) dated 25/1/2006
35. Letter No.11/2(A)/2004/SP-TBL/263 dated 14/2/2005
36. Common term referring to a member of armed opposition group
37. Letter No. 11/2(A)/04/SP-TBL/2075 dated 14/6/04
38. Letter No. 11/2(A)/2004/SP-TBL/2521 dated 20/12/04
39. Letter No. 17/13/2000-S(SW)
40. Letter No. 17/3/2000-S(SW) dated 1/3/2001
41. Letter No.2/12(13)/2004-H(MHRC) dated 23/7/2004
42. Letter No. 15/524/2004/HR/PHQ/522 dated 23/7/2004.
43. Letter No. 6/20/SSP-IW/2003(Pt-26)/2506 dated 26/5/2003
44. Letter No. 11/2(A)/04/SP TBL /184 dated 1/2/2005
45. *Newsletter*, AHRC, Vol.1 No. 1 (January 1997) and Annual Report, AHRC, 1996-97.

46. *Newsletter,* MHRC, Vol.1 No.1 (10th May 1999).
47. *Newsletter,* AHRC, Vol.1 No. 1 (January 1997) and Annual Report, AHRC, 1996-97.
48. *Newsletter,* MHRC, Vol.1 No.1 (10th May 1999).
49. Arun Ray Mohapatra, *op.cit.,* p.146.
50. *Newsletter,* AHRC, Vol.1 No. 1 (January 1997), News letter, AHRC, Vol.2 No. 1 (November 2000), Annual Report, AHRC, 1996-97 and documents collected from AHRC.
51. *Newsletter*, MHRC, Vol.1 No.1 (10th May 1999), News Letter, MHRC, Vol.2 No. 1 (10th December 2006) and documents collected from MHRC.
52. *Newsletter*, AHRC, Vol.2 No. 1 (November 2000)
53. Letter No. AHRC(CMA) 297/278 dated 13/9/99
54. Vide Letter No. AHRC(CMA) 97/267 dated 2/7/99
55. News Letter, AHRC, Vol.2 No. 1 (November 2000)
56. Letter no. AHRC (CMA) 97/285 dated 11/10/99
57. *Newsletter*, MHRC, Vol.1 No.1 (10th May 1999)

4

Interface between State Human Rights Commission and Non-Governmental Organizations

The importance of Non-Governmental Organizations (NGOs) in the field of human rights is widely recognized irrespective of whether it is international or national or local. As these organizations are in close contact with the grass root level people and have knowledge about the situation; hence they can contribute positively towards building the human rights awareness among the people they are working with. The National Human Rights Commission also underlines the importance of keeping contact with the NGOs. According to the Protection of Human Rights Act 1993 [Section 12(i)] both NHRC and different SHRCs are required to "encourage the efforts of non governmental organization and institutions working in the field of human rights."

In this chapter an attempt has been made to examine the workings of NGOs in Assam and Manipur with special emphasis on their relation with their State Commissions and the perception of these NGOs regarding the State Human Rights Commission of their respective states. 7 (Seven) NGOs from Assam and 12 (twelve) from Manipur have been selected for the study.

There are number of NGOs working in Assam and Manipur which are actively engaged in the propagation and promotion of human rights. However, there are few such organizations which are in constant interaction with the NHRC and SHRC. The relationship of NGOs with the NHRC and SHRC has been considered in selecting them. The Secretaries/Coordinators/

Directors as the case may be were interviewed to elicit their opinion on their activities and their relationship with both the NHRC and SHRC.

Objectives of NGOs under Study

The following are the common objectives of the selected NGOs in Assam and Manipur-

- spreading human rights awareness;
- monitoring and protecting rights of victims;
- to create a just society where people can live with dignity;
- to remove conflict and bring peace in the society;
- honour and protect identities of all communities;
- to develop programmes for self employment;
- to develop social and economic condition of people;
- achieve society free from HIV/AIDS;
- work for recognition of right to self determination;
- to protect the state terrorism.

There are different activities, undertaken by the NGOs in Assam and Manipur during the last ten years. Among them some are-

- publication of magazines like '*Manipur Update*' by the NGO Human Rights Alert, newsletters, journals, leaflets/ booklets, books. NGOs also contribute articles in several other journals; publish posters, stickers, paper clippings on different issues in order to aware people about rights and also about activities of their own NGOs.
- organizing workshops for spreading awareness among the people about human rights;
- filing cases on behalf of the victims to respective SHRCs, National Human Rights Commission, and Asian Human Rights Commission etc;

- instituting independent fact findings Commissions ;
- to do capacity building programmes for NGOs on human rights;
- research and documentations on human rights violations;
- organizing movements for maintaining territorial integrity of Manipur and repeal of AFSPA in case of Manipur NGOs;
- organizing awareness programmes on HIV/AIDS, educational programmes for HIV/AIDS infected children, health programmes etc;
- training programmes (vocational training programmes on embroidery, tailoring etc.) for capacity building and self employment.

Before dealing with the views of NGOs regarding the role of their respective SHRCs it is necessary to analyze the functioning of NGOs and their achievements so far as the fulfillment of the objective is concerned. Data presented below have been collected by interviewing respondents with schedule.

Fulfillment of Objectives of the Organization

The efficacy of any organizations depends on their ability to fulfill their objectives. From the following Table 4.1 it is seen achievement of objectives is higher in Assam than in Manipur. In case of Assam 85.71% NGOs opined that they are able to fulfill their objectives and only 14.29% NGOs partly fulfill their objectives. Whereas in case of Manipur only 58.33% NGOs agreed that their organizations are able to meet the objectives and 41.67% say that they are able to do so only partly.

Table- 4.1
Percentage showing the fulfillment of objectives by the NGOs in Assam & Manipur

Able to Fulfill Objectives	*Assam*	*Manipur*
Yes	85.71	58.33
No	Nil	Nil
Partly	14.29	41.67

It implies that the percentage of NGOs which fulfilled their objectives is much higher in Assam than Manipur. However, the respondents cited various reasons for their inability to fulfill the objectives, such as 'lack of resources and man power, non co-operation by the authorities, ethnic clashes, lack of coordination with other organizations, armed conflict situation, divide and rule policy of Govt. of India among the ethnic communities of Manipur-violation, suppression, colonization.

Frequency of Organizing Awareness Programmes

NGOs publish newsletters, journals, leaflets/booklets and books etc. NGO personals publish posters, stickers, paper clippings on different issues in order to aware people about rights and also about activities of their respective NGOs and also contribute articles in several journals.

Further in order to spread awareness among people about human rights and also about various means for protecting their rights in cases of violations, NGOs conduct seminars, workshops, training programmes, orientation programmes, meetings, contact programmes, street plays etc.

Although all these NGOs claim to organize awareness campaign, there is no uniformity in the frequency of organizing these programmes as seen from the Table 4.2 presented below.

Table - 4.2

Percentage showing the frequency of the Awareness Programmes organized by the NGOs in Manipur and Assam

Frequency	*Assam*	*Manipur*
Regularly	28.57	33.33
Once in a Month	Nil	16.67
Twice in a Year	14.29	8.33
Some times	28.57	8.33
As per Necessity	28.57	25
No Answer	Nil	8.33

Table 4.2 shows that in Assam 28.57% NGOs said that they organize awareness programmes regularly; 14.29% NGOs opined that they organize these twice in a year and 28.57% NGOs said they organize such programme only some times and equal percentage of NGOs said it is as per necessity. In Manipur, 33.33% NGOs organize awareness programmes regularly whereas only 8.33% of NGOs said they organize the programme twice a year; another 8.33% NGOs opined that they conduct it some times, 16.67% NGOs organize once a month and 25% NGOs organize this as per necessity. 8.33% organizations in Manipur did not respond.

Efficacy of protest march and such other Programmes

When the violations of human rights take place NGOs take up protest marches, silent marches through the place, *gheraoing* offices of law enforcing agencies, calls strikes/blockades, use legal mechanisms, take up advocacy programmes, demonstration in front of public authority offices etc. for protesting against the violation. There are no two opinions regarding the efficacy of these protests in resolving the problem although not all problems can be solved through such activities as seen from the following table. Respondents agree that owing to the protests by these organizations up to 30% cases are resolved.

Table- 4.3

Percentage showing results of the protests organized by the NGOs in Manipur & Assam

Result of these Protests	*Assam*	*Manipur*
10-30% cases are solved	28.57	50
31-50% cases are solved	14.29	8.33
51-70% cases are solved	——	——
71-90% cases are solved	28.57	—
Never Solved	Nil	8.33

Table 4.3 shows that in Assam among the NGOs 28.57% feel that as a result of these protests 10% to 30% cases are solved;

another 28.57% think that 71-90% cases are solved; only 14.29% think that 31%to 50% cases are solved because of their action and another 28.57% do not give any answer. Whereas in case of Manipur among various NGOs 50% opined that as a result of these protests 10% to 30% cases are solved; 8.33% viewed that 31%to 50% cases are solved. Another 8.33% think that the cases are never solved and 33.34% do not give any answer.

From this we can infer that the NGOs of Assam hold much positive view on the efficacy of protest against the violation of human rights than NGOs of Manipur.

Contact with international/ national organizations and personalities

All the NGOs of both the states have contacts with national/ international personalities through email/internet, personnel contact/telephone, meetings, joint programmes etc. These organizations have also contacts with state, national and international level NGOs.

In Assam, 57.14% of the respondents have regular contacts with national/international level personalities and other NGOs; 28.57% sometimes maintain contacts and 14.29% maintain contacts once in a year, as shown in table- 4.4. All of the NGOs in Assam think that such contacts help them in reaching out their goals. The case of Manipur is not so much different so far as regularity is concerned. Among the NGOs, 58.33% maintain regular contacts with national/international level personalities and other NGOs; and 41.67% maintain such contacts sometimes, indicated in Table- 4.4.

Table- 4.4

Percentage showing the Nature of Contacts of the NGOs with state/national/international level NGOs

Nature of Contact	*Assam*	*Manipur*
Regular	57.14	58.33
Sometimes	28.57	41.67
Once in a Year	14.29	—
As per Necessity	Nil	Nil

It is found that in Assam more or less all human rights NGOs maintain contact with national/international personalities and state/national/ international level NGOs. And the noticeable point is that majority of them maintain contacts regularly. But the situation of Manipur shows that majority of the NGOs maintain contacts with national/international personalities for their own work only.

Nature of relation between the NGOs and Government

Table - 4.5 shows that among the NGOs in Assam 14.29% always approach the Government for the solution of their problems; 57.14% quite often approach government for this purpose whereas 28.57% never approach the government for solution of their problems. The table also shows that among the NGOs in Manipur 25% always approach the Government for the solution of their problems; 66.67% quite often approach government for that purpose whereas 8.33% never approach government for their problem solution.

In the study we tried to understand that how the relationship between the NGOs and the Government helps in finding solutions to their (NGOs) problems. It showed that in both states majority of the NGOs approach the Government quite often.

Table- 4.5

Percentage showing NGOs in Manipur & Assam who approach the Government for Solution of Problems

Frequency	*Assam*	*Manipur*
Always	14.29	25
Quite often	57.14	66.67
Not at all	28.57	8.33

A comparative study of the above table shows that in both the states NGOs approach the government quite often. NGOs in Manipur appear to contact more frequently than the NGOs in Assam as we can see from the above table that 28.57% of respondents in Assam said that they never approach the government whereas it is only 8.33% in case of Manipur.

Those who approach government for the solution of their problems they approach the ruling political party, maintain close contact with the minister concerned and also approach the officials in the department as the means of access to the Government.

Government's Response towards NGOs

In Assam majority of NGOs (57.14%) opined that government's response is poor towards them; 14.29% opined that there is very good response from government towards them; another 14.29% opined that government response is good, and 14.29% did not give any answer (Table- 4.6). In case of Manipur 41.67% opined that government response is poor; 33.33% opined that there is good response from government towards them; 8.33% say that government response is very good, and 8.33% viewed that the response is hostile. Another 8.33% did not give any answer.

Table- 4.6
Percentage showing the Government Response towards NGOs in Assam & Manipur

Government Response towards NGOs	*Assam*	*Manipur*
Good	14.29	33.33
Very Good	14.29	8.33
No Response	Nil	Nil
Poor	57.14	41.67
Hostile	Nil	8.33
No Answer	14.29	8.33

The response of the Government towards NGOs in case of Assam is poor. And this is the view of majority of NGOs of this state. Similar view is expressed by maximum NGOs of Manipur.

Interface between SHRCs and NGOs

NGOs in Assam have contacts with Assam Human Rights Commission. As indicated in table- 4.7 among NGOs 85.71% have contacts with AHRC whereas 14.29% replied in negative. The case of Manipur is also not much different from Assam. 91.67% of NGOs in Manipur have contacts with MHRC whereas only 8.33% replied in negative. The detail is shown in table-4.7.

Table- 4.7

NGOs Contact with SHRC

Maintain Contact with SHRC	*Assam*	*Manipur*
Yes	85.71	91.67
No	14.29	8.33

In Assam 71.43% of selected NGOs viewed that maintaining contact with AHRC helps them in their work. 14.29% thinks that such contacts sometimes prove helpful to them and another 14.29% did not give any answer (table- 4.8). In case of Manipur 50% of NGOs think that maintaining contact with MHRC helps them in their work; 41.67% NGOs think it is only sometimes whereas 8.33% think that such contacts do not help them. (Table- 4.8)

Table - 4.8

Maintaining Contacts that Helps NGOs

Maintaining Contact Helps the NGO	*Assam*	*Manipur*
Yes	71.43	50
Sometimes	14.29	41.67
No	Nil	8.33
No Answer	14.29	——

In this area of providing helps AHRC is in better position than MHRC. NGOs received help from SHRCs in conducting seminars, workshops, conferences, in filing cases, in human rights campaign, in providing information on human rights related issues, free legal aid service etc. The SHRC members also individually co-operate with NGOs.

As NGOs are engaged in grass root level works naturally their views are important in several cases. Table- 4.9 shows that in Assam 57.14% NGOs agreed that AHRC intimate them for discussion/suggestions in human rights violation issues whereas remaining 28.57% replied negatively and 12.5% did not give any answer. The table also shows that among the NGOs in Manipur 58.33% viewed that MHRC intimate them for discussion/ suggestions in human rights violation issues and 41.67% replied negatively.

Table- 4.9

SHRC's intimation with NGOs for discussions/ suggestions

SHRC intimate for discussion/suggestion	*Assam*	*Manipur*
Yes	57.14	58.33
No	28.57	41.67
No Answer	14.29	—

Table 4.9 clearly shows that regarding intimation for discussion/suggestion by the SHRCs views of NGOs in both Assam and Manipur are almost similar in the positive side. It is also important to mention here one thing which came out during the interviews that both in Assam and Manipur NGOs are intimated by respective SHRCs only in particular cases related to them.

Those who responded positively in case of Assam among them 50% say that they are intimated sometimes and another 50% viewed that they are intimated as per necessity, indicated in table 4.10. Among the respondent NGOs of Manipur 42.86% viewed that they are intimated sometimes; another 42.86% viewed that they are intimated as per necessity whereas 14.28% say that they are regularly intimated (Table- 4.10).

Table- 4.10
Nature of Contact by SHRC

Nature of Contact by SHRC	*Assam*	*Manipur*
Regular	Nil	14.28
Some times	50	42.86
As per Necessity	50	42.86

The above table shows that in case of Assam NGOs are sharply divided in two equal parts in this question. The figures also indicate that there is no practice of consulting the NGOs by the AHRC on a regular basis. But the case of Manipur clearly shows that a few NGOs are intimated by MHRC for discussion/ suggestion on a regular basis.

Regarding the performance of the AHRC 42.85% viewed that AHRC is working properly; 28.57% think that it is not working properly. Among the NGOs14.29% think that the functioning of AHRC is pro-government and another14.29% does not give any response (table- 4.11). But the case of Manipur shows that, regarding the performance of the MHRC 25% NGOs think that it is working properly; 41.67% think that it is not working properly, another 25% viewed that the functioning of MHRC is Pro-government and 8.33% do not give any response, indicated in Table-4.11.

Table- 4.11

Performance of SHRC

Rating of Performance of SHRC	*Assam*	*Manipur*
Working Properly	42.85	25
Not working Properly	28.57	41.67
Pro-government working	14.29	25
No Answer	14.29	8.33

It indicates that the workings of the AHRC are proper as expressed by the maximum of NGOS in Assam. But the case of Manipur is different; only one fourth of the NGOs think that MHRC is working properly whereas majority of them said that the MHRC is not working properly; moreover it works in favour of the government.

The basic shortcomings of the Assam Human Rights Commission as cited by NGOs of Assam are-

- lack of independence in financial matters;
- lack of infrastructure and independent investigation team of its own;
- delay in disposing cases;
- lack in utilizing power and force;
- existence of AHRC is not known to general people;
- inability to take action, can only recommend for it;
- attitude of the Chairperson and Members seem to be pro-government.

The basic shortcomings of the Manipur Human Rights Commission as indicated by NGOs of Manipur are-

- members are either ineffective or are appointed on political consideration;
- use of MHRC by the government;
- lack of infrastructure and expertise among the staff members;
- delay of work proceedings;
- concerned with civil rights only;
- state government does not comply with the recommendations of MHRC;
- there is no secretary and investigation team;
- no woman member in MHRC;
- hikes of salary of members depends on state government.

SHRCs and Political Interference

On the question of level of political interference in the working SHRCs majority of the NGOs (57.14%) said that there is no political interference from the government in the workings of AHRC; 42.86% of the NGOs in Assam agreed that there is political interference from the government in the functioning of AHRC. But in case of Manipur a large section of the NGOs (83.33%) think that there is political interference in the workings of MHRC, only 8.33% disagreed with this view and another 8.33% did not give any answer.

Table- 4.12
Political Interference from Government

Political Interference from Government	*Assam*	*Manipur*
Yes	42.86	83.33
No	57.14	8.33
No Answer	Nil	8.33

It indicates that there is less political interference from Government in workings of SHRC of Assam than the SHRC of Manipur.

SHRC as Defender of Human Rights

On the question of SHRC as the defender of human rights 42.86% NGOs opined that AHRC's role is good; another 42.86% NGOs are of the view that AHRC's role is poor and 14.28% viewed that it is very poor in this regard. Viewed in its totality we find that the majority of NGOs in Assam find the role of AHRC as defender of human rights poor. But we find different picture so far as the perceptions of the NGOs in Manipur are concerned. 58.33% viewed that its role is good; 33.33% viewed that it is poor and 8.33% viewed that it is very poor (Table- 4.13).

Table- 4.13

Role of SHRC as Defender of Human Rights

Role of SHRC as Defender of human Rights	*Assam*	*Manipur*
Good	42.86	58.33
Poor	42.86	33.33
Very Poor	14.28	8.33

It can be understood that in Assam the role of AHRC as the defender of human rights is neither too satisfactory nor too hopeless as the percentage of NGOs that viewed its role as good and poor are equal, i.e., 42.86%. But the situation of Manipur is little better than Assam. More than half of NGOs opined that MHRC's role as defender of human rights is good.

Any organization is established to fulfill some basic objectives. Regarding the objectives of AHRC, 42.86% of NGOs opined that AHRC is not able to fulfill its objectives whereas 57.14% viewed that AHRC partially fulfilled the objectives, indicated in table- 4.14. The table also shows that only 8.33% NGOs in Manipur think that MHRC fulfilled its objectives, 25% opined that it is not able to fulfill its objectives whereas 66.67% viewed that it has partially fulfilled the objectives.

Table- 4.14
NGOs perception on SHRC

Fulfilled its objectives	*Assam*	*Manipur*
Yes	Nil	8.33
No	42.86	25.00
Partially	57.14	66.67

It indicates that maximum NGOs of both states viewed that their SHRCs have fulfilled their (SHRC's) objectives partially. In case of Manipur a few NGOs think that MHRC has fulfilled its objectives.

It may be noted here that the NGOs we have selected for the purpose of the present study consists of those organizations which work in the field of human rights and are active at the grass root level. According to our findings, majority of these organizations do not get support from the government. The organizations are well aware of the role and significance of the SHRCs and feel that contact with their respective SHRC helps them in their works. But they are not very categorical about the positive role and performance of these Commissions. As we have seen above that in case of Manipur majority of the NGOs (66.67%) feel that MHRC has fulfilled its objectives partially; only one- fourth of the NGOs replied in negative. In case of Assam we find that 57.14% feel that AHRC has fulfilled its objectives partially; 42.86% mention that in their opinion the AHRC has failed to fulfill its objectives. We find a reflection of their assessment in their answer on the role of SHRC as defender of human rights. Majority of the respondents in Assam feel that track record of AHRC as defender of human rights is poor whereas 42.86% feel it's good. On the contrary majority of NGOs feel that their role in defending the rights of the people is good; only 41.33% judge them as poor performer. Finally, in Assam NGOs think that AHRC is working in a political interference free atmosphere whereas the situation of Manipur is just the opposite.

In order to ensure the protection of the rights of the people the human rights organization has an important role to play. This calls for a concerted effort on the part of both the Government and NGOs. The achievement of the goal of ensuring human rights will become possible if there is a close interrelationship among these organizations. Our study on Assam and Manipur indicate that they are yet to achieve this kind of interface.

5

Conclusion

It is seen that human beings, irrespective of any kind of discrimination, are entitled to certain basic rights which are primary requisite for the development of their inherent dignity; these rights are basically recognized by the state and in general they are called human rights. This concept of human rights achieved momentum after the adoption of UDHR and got legal sanction with the adoption of ICCPR and ICESCR, the provisions of which are similar to the Indian Constitution and several other acts adopted by the Parliament. Besides Constitutional provisions India also adopted the Protection of Human Rights Act 1993 which is the major milestone in the protection of human rights.

The Protection of Human Rights Act 1993 was adopted after a series of guidelines set forth by the UN seminar, international and national pressures like movements of APDR, ACLC; violation of human rights during emergency period and recommendations of Minorities Commission, 1983 etc. In this backdrop in 1992 Chief Ministers' Committee was established along with other Central Ministers to set out the guidelines for the establishment of NHRC and SHRCs. Accordingly in 1993 the Protection of Human Rights Act was passed and came into force on 28th September 1993. As per the Act AHRC and MHRC have been established in Assam and Manipur respectively which was much needed at that time. In both Assam and Manipur there have been gross violations of human rights due to the insurgency and counter insurgency operations. It creates a lot of hardship towards the full achievement of basic rights of people. Naturally the role of SHRCs in these states is very significant as governmental machinery to protect the rights of common mass. The following points give us an idea about the workings of the State Human Rights Commissions of Northeast India and also the views of non-governmental organizations regarding the role of these Commissions.

Assessment

- The existence of insurgency and counter-insurgency operations has made the human rights situations of North east India especially in Assam and Manipur very grim. The establishment of the AHRC and MHRC in Assam and Manipur respectively was not only in keeping with the provisions of the Protection of Human Rights Act 1993 but was an urgent need of time.
- The division of works of both these state Commissions are not clear. In AHRC three members including the Chairperson and fourteen (14) administrative staffs has been discharging functions. But incase of MHRC there exist four members including the Chairperson as they were appointed prior to the amendment of the Act, in 2006[1] and every year a new batch of staff is deputed from other departments of the government to hold office except the Deputy Secretary who has been there for long time. Presently, fourteen deputed employees are discharging functions in the office of MHRC.
- Till date AHRC does not have its own secretary. The present incumbent is an I.A.S Officer who looks after the works of the AHRC as an additional charge. Owing to this it is not possible for him to attend the office of the AHRC every day. The MHRC also does not have secretary till date. There is one deputy secretary; he is the Deputy Secretary to the Govt. of Manipur, Department of Law; and has the additional charge of MHRC.
- The AHRC and MHRC do not have their own investigation teams. The present staffs of investigation team of AHRC have the additional charge of AHRC with their regular duties in the police department. The SHRCs have been constituted mainly to see that the rights of the people are protected and not violated and if such violations take place then victims should get justice. But without independent

investigation team objective results cannot be ensured especially in cases of alleged human rights violation perpetrated by police officials/ armed personnels.

- Both the SHRCs are functioning as machinery for protection and promotion of human rights of the people. In this process SHRCs have actively registered many cases of human rights violations since their inception. After analyzing the role of both the Commissions it is found that since 1996 to 31st March, 2007 i.e., since its establishment to 31st March, 2007 AHRC has registered and disposed 6189 and 4684 cases respectively. And in case of MHRC (since its establishment in 2000 to 31st December 2007) the number of registered and disposed cases are 1163 and 599 respectively. The study further shows that in both AHRC and MHRC the numbers of cases registered and disposed started decreasing after the initial years of establishment. This indicates the declining trend of people's faith on these organizations as the defender of human rights.
- Both AHRC and MHRC covered several aspects of cases relating to violation of human rights. These include cases of disappearances, rape, custodial deaths, irregularity of basic services etc.
- It is an important function of SHRCs to make people aware about their rights and also about the available mechanisms for their protection if those rights are violated. AHRC conducted many awareness programs like seminars, training programmes, discussions, orientation programme for making people conscious about their human rights. But it is found that the initial enthusiasm in spreading awareness by conducting seminars, training programmes, orientation programmes has been decreasing. This indicates gradual decrease of AHRC's functioning. For spreading human rights awareness MHRC also conducted similar programs like AHRC. MHRC's plan indicates that this would be done in a phased manner starting from district level and going down to the village. Till the time

of the collection of data, it has completed the programme at the district level. The process is going on in an organized way.

- An important function of SHRCs is to undertake and promote research in the field of human rights [section 12(7)]. Between 1998 and 1999 the AHRC completed two UNICEF projects. But after this no research project has been undertaken by AHRC. MHRC has not undertaken a single research project yet although it is required in 12 (g) of the Act of 1993.
- According to the provisions of the Act the state commissions are required to submit their activities in detail including the financial report to the respective state governments which will place it before the State Legislature. These reports are open to all Members of the Legislature for scrutiny and comments [section 28(1) (2)]. AHRC so far has placed two reports to the Assam Government i.e. annual report of 1996-97 and annual reports from 1997-2002. But only one i.e. annual report of 1996-97 so far has been placed before the legislature and was passed. The MHRC has not placed a single annual report before the state government. This hampers the SHRCs accountability towards legislature and indicates major lack of efficiency on the part of both the SHRCs and also the state governments.
- So far as the finance is concerned the state government releases money to MHRC according to its submitted proposal, but this does not happen in case of AHRC. The government of Assam so far has released less than 50% of the proposed amount by the AHRC.
- According to article 35(2) of the Act, the finance of SHRC should be audited by Comptroller and Auditor General or any other person appointed by him. But till date audit of the accounts of both AHRC and MHRC has not been done. It indicates lack of interest on the part of both the governments on the activities of their respective Commissions. Apart from this, such a situation puts a

question mark on the financial discipline of the AHRC and MHRC.

- Since its establishment AHRC has not performed the following two functions [section 12 (d) and (e)]:

1. reviewing the safeguards provided by or under the Constitution or any law for the time being in force for the protection of human rights and recommend measures for their effective implementation,[section (d)];
2. reviewing the factors, including acts of terrorism that inhibit the enjoyment of human rights and recommending appropriate remedial measures, [section (e)];

The MHRC too has not performed the above mentioned two functions.

Although the AHRC and MHRC have been assigned a number of functions they are not undertaking all the functions as seen from above discussions. In recent times, the acts of terrorism have shown upward trend and are the nastiest means for violation of human rights but the lack of AHRC and MHRC's concern in these matters raises serious question regarding the efficacy of these organizations.

The members of AHRC have visited a number of jails, police stations throughout the state. On the basis of these visits the then Chairperson Sri Justice S.N. Bhargava made several recommendations to the Chief Minister of Assam for improving the hygienic conditions of jails, for the supply of medicines to prisoners and essential repairs of the staff quarters was also recommended. The Commission also visited custodial homes, hospitals, relief camps. MHRC too visited custodial homes, hospitals, relief camps, central jails, blind School, deaf and dumb School etc of the state to examine the living conditions of people there.

In analyzing the role of the SHRCS, opinions of NGOs are very important as they are the human rights activists at the grass root level. It is found that majority of these organizations (NGOs) do not get support from the government. The organizations are aware of the functions and importance of SHRCs and acknowledged that maintaining contact with their respective SHRCs can help them in their works. But they are not very categorical about the positive role and performance of these Commissions. In case of Manipur majority of the NGOs (66.67%) feel that MHRC has fulfilled its objectives partially; only one- fourth of the NGOs replied negatively in this respect. In case of Assam we find that (57.14%) feel that AHRC has fulfilled its objectives partially; and 42.86% mention that the AHRC has failed to fulfill its objectives. And majority of the NGOs in Assam feel that track record of AHRC as defender of human rights is poor whereas 42.86% feel it's good. On the contrary majority of them feel that their role in defending the rights of the people is good. Only 41.33% judge them as poor performer. Finally, in Assam NGOs think that AHRC is working in an atmosphere free from political interference whereas the situation of Manipur is just the opposite one.

In protection of the rights of common people both SHRCs and NGOs have important role to play. For this the close relationship between them (SHRCs and NGOs) is the primary requirement. Both in Assam and Manipur this kind of interface are yet to achieve.

Recommendations

There are certain areas of functioning in case of both AHRC & MHRC which need to be addressed earnestly. These are presented below:

1. **Speedy disposal of cases:** Both AHRC and MHRC should dispose the already registered cases of human rights violations as early as possible. And in disposing cases Commissions should be neutral.
2. **Need to fill up the vacant positions**: Commissions should look at its strength which lies in the officials. They should not keep any post vacant.
3. **Mechanisms for adequate funding**: Government should provide adequate finance. Without a strong financial background Commissions cannot perform some of its functions properly like awareness campaigns, seminars etc.

4. **Regular publication of annual reports**: Commissions must submit annual reports on their activities and financial reports to their respective state governments regularly in order to show their efficiency, commitment and sincerity towards the fulfillment of their objectives.

5. **Stress on research projects**: Commissions must undertake and promote more and more researches in the field of human rights.

6. **Government's non-interference and political pressure**: The government of the day should desist from exerting political pressure on the appointment of Commission members and allow them autonomy in discharging their duties.

7. **Close coordination between the SHRCs and NGOs:** NGOs which are working in the field of human rights should be involved in the workings of Commissions. Their advice and experience may go a long way in revamping the work of these Commissions.

Unless the Commission can actively work towards the propagation, promotion and protection of rights of the people as provided in the Protection of Human Rights Act 1993, its functioning will be no different from any government department which are characterized by red tapism, absence of orientation, paucity of fund, vacant position and so on. Our study of the State Human Rights Commissions in two states has shown that there is much to be done if SHRC has to fully realize its objectives and goals.

NOTE

1. According to the amendment effected in 2006 the State Commission shall, with effect from such date as the State Government may by notification specify, consists of- a) a Chairperson who has been a Chief Justice of a High Court; b) one Member who is, or has been, a Judge of a High Court or District Judge in the State with a minimum of seven years experience as District Judge; c) one Member to be appointed from amongst persons having knowledge of, or practical experience in, matters relating to human rights. Subs. By Act, 43 of 2006

Select Bibliography

Books, Articles

Ansari, M.R., *Protecting Human Rights.* Maxford Books, New Delhi, 2006.

Basu, Durga Das, *Introduction to the Constitution of India.* Wadhwa and Company Law Publishers, Agra, 2004.

Bhattacharjee, Chinmayee, *An Interface between Insurgency and Human Rights in Northeast India.* M.Phil Diss., Assam University, 2004.

Bhattacharjee, Tanmoy, *Political Economy of North-East India.* Self Published, Assam, 2004.

Dhamala, Ranju R., "Human Rights: Problems and Challenges", *Assam University Journal. A journal of New Ideas,* vol.1 no.1 (January 2006).

Dhamala, Ranju R. and Sukalpa Bhattacharjee (eds.), *Human Rights and Insurgency: The North-East India.* Shipra Publications, New Delhi, 2002.

Jaswal, Dr. Paramjit S. and Dr. Nishtha Jaswal, *Human Rights And The Law.* APH Publishing Corporation, New Delhi, 1996.

Jayapalan, N., *Human Rights.* Atlantic Publishers and Distributors, New Delhi, 2000

Kalita, Paramananda, Subhram Rajkhowa, Sheikh Chand Mohammad, *The International Bill of Human Rights.* Assam Human Rights Commission, Assam, 2001

Krome, Neingulo, "Human Rights Movement in Nagaland", in Naorem Sanajaoba(ed.), *Human Rights: Principles, Practices and Abuses.* Omsons Publications, New Delhi, 1994.

Mahanta, Aparna (ed.), *Human Rights and Women of North-East India.* Centre for Women's Studies, Dibrugarh University, Dibrugarh, 2002.

Manik Chakraborty, "Refugees and Human Rights -A case study of Chittagong Hill Tracts" in Naorem Sanajaoba (ed.), *Human Rights: Principles, Practices and Abuses.* Omsons Publications, New Delhi, 1994.

MASS, "Human Rights Violation in Assam (Operation Rhino, 1991)", in Naorem Sanajaoba(ed.), ·*Human Rights: Principles, Practices and Abuses.* Omsons Publications, New Delhi, 1994.

Mohapatra, Arun Roy, *National Human Rights Commission of India –Formation, Functioning and Future Prospects.* Radha Publications, New Delhi, 2001.

Nayar, Kuldip, *"Human Rights Violation in North East India." The Hindu*, (22nd May, 1997).

Nirmal, C. J. (ed.), *Human Rights in India – Historical, Social and Political Perspective.* Institute of Indian and International Studies, Oxford University Press, New Delhi, 2000.

O'Byrne, Darren J., *Human Rights – An Introduction.* Pearson Education, Singapore, Indian Branch, Delhi, 2004.

Sanajaoba, Naorem(ed.), *Human Rights: Principles, Practices and Abuses.* Omsons Publications, New Delhi, 1994.

Serto, Leban, *Documentation of Organizations/Individuals working in the field of Peace Building and Peace related issue in the State of Manipur, India.* Centre for Peace Education Manipur, Manipur in collaboration with AMAN Charitable Trust, New Delhi, 2007.

Sharma, Gokulesh, *Human Rights and Social Justice.* Deep & Deep Publications, New Delhi, 1998.

Singh, N. Nimai, "Human Rights Abuses by Security Forces in Manipur", in Sanajaoba, Naorem(ed.), *Human Rights: Principles, Practices and Abuses.* Omsons Publications, New Delhi, 1994.

Subramanian, S., *Human Rights: International Challenges.* Manas Publications, New Delhi, 1997.

Tandon, M.P. &. V.K Anand, *International Law & Human Rights.* Allahabad Law Agency, Haryana, 2004.

Vadkar, Praveen, *Concept, Theories and Practice of Human Rights.* Rajat Publications, New Delhi, 2000.

Internet Sources

Official website of Assam Human Rights Commission www.ahrc.gov.in

Official website of National Human Rights Commission www.nhrc.nic.in

Universal Declaration of Human Rights, http://www.un.org/en/documents/udhr/

Charter of the United Nations, http://www.un.org/en/documents/charter/preamble.shtml

Armed Forces Special Power Act, of 1958, *www.mha.nic.in/pdfs/armed_forces_special_powers_act1958.pdf*

Reports of Asian Centre for Human Rights; India Human Rights Report-2007, http://www.achrweb.org/reports/india/AR07/AR2007.htm

South Asia Terrorism Portal, www.satp.org

Fact Sheet No. 19, National Institutions for the Promotion and Protection of Human Rights, www.ohchr.org/Documents/Publications/FactSheet19en.pdf

Other Sources

Newsletter, Assam Human Rights Commission, Vol.1, No.1 (January, 1997)

Newsletter, Assam Human Rights Commission, Vol.2, No.1 (November, 2000)

Annual Report, Assam Human Rights Commission, 1996-97

News Letter, Manipur Human Rights Commission, Vol.1, No.1 (10th May, 1999)

News Letter, Manipur Human Rights Commission,Vol.2, Issue 1 (10th December, 2006)

MHRC, 'Know Manipur Human Rights Commission' (Leaflet)

Appendices

APPENDIX I
Annual Fatalities in Terrorist Violence in Assam, 1992-2008*

	Civilians	*Security Force Personnel*	*Terrorists*	*Total*
1992	80	34	19	133
1993	74	24	33	131
1994	173	35	63	271
1995	170	73	27	270
1996	302	87	62	451
1997	285	85	167	537
1998	531	72	180	783
1999	214	77	212	503
2000	366	65	327	758
2001	264	59	283	606
2002	138	32	275	445
2003	212	12	281	505
2004	194	24	136	354
2005	149	10	83	242
2006	96	35	43	174
2007	269	19	149	437
2008	207	16	122	345
Total	3724	759	2462	6945

* *Source*: South Asia Terrorism Portal www.satp.org

APPENDIX II

Annual Fatalities in Terrorist Violence in Manipur, 1992-2008*

	Civilians	*Security Force Personnel*	*Terrorists*	*Total*
1992	84	30	51	165
1993	266	91	66	423
1994	189	98	63	350
1995	183	64	74	321
1996	117	65	93	275
1997	233	111	151	495
1998	87	62	95	244
1999	89	64	78	231
2000	93	51	102	246
2001	70	25	161	256
2002	36	53	101	190
2003	27	23	148	198
2004	50	41	127	218
2005	138	50	143	331
2006	107	37	141	285
2007	150	40	218	408
2008	117	13	278	408
Total	2050	918	2087	5037

* *Source: South Asia Terrorism Portal www.satp.org*

APPENDIX III

District-wise Statement of Cases Registered (2003-2007) in AHRC

Sl.No	*District*	*2003-04*	*2004-05*	*2005-06*	*2006-07*
1.	Barpeta	15	5	11	16
2.	Bongaigaon	10	8	3	4
3.	Baska	-	-	3	2
4.	Cachar	25	38	47	44
5.	Chirang	-	-	1	1
6.	Dhubri	12	4	11	9
7.	Dhemaji	6	4	2	3
8.	Dibrugarh	24	20	41	16
9.	Darrang	50	18	17	13
10.	Goalpara	2	6	2	1
11.	Golaghat	13	7	18	8
12.	Hailakandi	12	7	14	13
13.	Jorhat	17	16	13	14
14.	Kokrajhar	17	14	2	3
15.	Kamrup	100	96	95	117
16.	Karbi Anglong	10	21	15	9
17.	Karimganj	20	24	18	15
18.	Lakhimpur	8	9	9	6
19.	Morigaon	7	8	10	10
20.	Nagaon	39	40	38	33
21.	N.C. Hills	2	-	-	6
22.	Nalbari	12	8	15	8
23.	Sibsagar	20	18	19	13
24.	Sonitpur	28	10	21	15
25.	Tinsukia	19	14	14	12
26.	Udalguri	-	8	4	4
27.	Outside the State	2	4	6	7
	Total -	470	407	449	402

* *Source:* Office of the Assam Human Rights Commission

APPENDIX IV

UNIVERSAL DECLARATION OF HUMAN RIGHTS

[Adopted and proclaimed by General Assembly of the United Nations on 10 December, 1948]

Preamble

Whereas recognition of the inherent dignity and of the equal and inalienable rights of all members of the human family is the foundation of freedom, justice and peace in the world,

Whereas disregard and contempt for human rights have resulted in barbarous acts which have outraged the conscience of mankind, and the advent of a world in which human beings shall enjoy freedom of speech and belief and freedom from fear and want has been proclaimed as the highest aspiration of the common people,

Whereas it is essential, if man is not to be compelled to have recourse, as a last resort, to rebellion against tyranny and oppression, that human rights should be protected by the rule of law,

Whereas it is essential to promote the development of friendly relations between nations,

Whereas the peoples of the United Nations have in the Charter reaffirmed their faith in fundamental human rights, in the dignity and worth of the human person and in the equal rights of men and women and have determined to promote social progress and better standards of life in larger freedom,

Whereas Member States have pledged themselves to achieve, in co-operation with the United Nations, the promotion of universal respect for and observance of human rights and fundamental freedoms,

Whereas a common understanding of these rights and freedoms is of the greatest importance for the full realization of this pledge,

Now, Therefore THE GENERAL ASSEMBLY proclaims THIS UNIVERSAL DECLARATION OF HUMAN RIGHTS as a common standard of achievement for all peoples and all nations, to the end that every individual and every organ of society, keeping this Declaration constantly in mind, shall strive by teaching and education to promote respect for these rights and freedoms and by progressive measures, national and international, to secure their universal and effective recognition and observance, both among the peoples of Member States themselves and among the peoples of territories under their jurisdiction.

Article 1

All human beings are born free and equal in dignity and rights.They are endowed with reason and conscience and should act towards one another in a spirit of brotherhood.

Article 2

Everyone is entitled to all the rights and freedoms set forth in this Declaration, without distinction of any kind, such as race, colour, sex, language, religion, political or other opinion, national or social origin, property, birth or other status. Furthermore, no distinction shall be made on the basis of the political, jurisdictional or international status of the country or territory to which a person belongs, whether it be independent, trust, non-self-governing or under any other limitation of sovereignty.

Article 3

Everyone has the right to life, liberty and security of person.

Article 4

No one shall be held in slavery or servitude; slavery and the slave trade shall be prohibited in all their forms.

Article 5

No one shall be subjected to torture or to cruel, inhuman or degrading treatment or punishment.

Article 6

Everyone has the right to recognition everywhere as a person before the law.

Article 7

All are equal before the law and are entitled without any

discrimination to equal protection of the law. All are entitled to equal protection against any discrimination in violation of this Declaration and against any incitement to such discrimination.

Article 8

Everyone has the right to an effective remedy by the competent national tribunals for acts violating the fundamental rights granted him by the constitution or by law.

Article 9

No one shall be subjected to arbitrary arrest, detention or exile.

Article 10

Everyone is entitled in full equality to a fair and public hearing by an independent and impartial tribunal, in the determination of his rights and obligations and of any criminal charge against him.

Article 11

(1) Everyone charged with a penal offence has the right to be presumed innocent until proved guilty according to law in a public trial at which he has had all the guarantees necessary for his defence.

(2) No one shall be held guilty of any penal offence on account of any act or omission which did not constitute a penal offence, under national or international law, at the time when it was committed. Nor shall a heavier penalty be imposed than the one that was applicable at the time the penal offence was committed.

Article 12

No one shall be subjected to arbitrary interference with his privacy, family, home or correspondence, nor to attacks upon his honour and reputation. Everyone has the right to the protection of the law against such interference or attacks.

Article 13

(1) Everyone has the right to freedom of movement and residence within the borders of each state.

(2) Everyone has the right to leave any country, including his own, and to return to his country.

Article 14

(1) Everyone has the right to seek and to enjoy in other countries asylum from persecution.

(2) This right may not be invoked in the case of prosecutions genuinely arising from non-political crimes or from acts contrary to the purposes and principles of the United Nations.

Article 15

(1) Everyone has the right to a nationality.

(2) No one shall be arbitrarily deprived of his nationality nor denied the right to change his nationality.

Article 16

(1) Men and women of full age, without any limitation due to race, nationality or religion, have the right to marry and to found a family. They are entitled to equal rights as to marriage, during marriage and at its dissolution.

(2) Marriage shall be entered into only with the free and full consent of the intending spouses.

(3) The family is the natural and fundamental group unit of society and is entitled to protection by society and the State.

Article 17

(1) Everyone has the right to own property alone as well as in association with others.

(2) No one shall be arbitrarily deprived of his property.

Article 18

Everyone has the right to freedom of thought, conscience and religion; this right includes freedom to change his religion or belief, and freedom, either alone or in community with others and in public or private, to manifest his religion or belief in teaching, practice, worship and observance.

Article 19

Everyone has the right to freedom of opinion and expression; this right includes freedom to hold opinions without interference and to seek, receive and impart information and ideas through any media and regardless of frontiers.

Article 20

(1) Everyone has the right to freedom of peaceful assembly and association.

(2) No one may be compelled to belong to an association.

Article 21

(1) Everyone has the right to take part in the government of his country, directly or through freely chosen representatives.

(2) Everyone has the right of equal access to public service in his country.

(3) The will of the people shall be the basis of the authority of government; this will shall be expressed in periodic and genuine elections which shall be by universal and equal suffrage and shall be held by secret vote or by equivalent free voting procedures.

Article 22

Everyone, as a member of society, has the right to social security and is entitled to realization, through national effort and international co-operation and in accordance with the organization and resources of each State, of the economic, social and cultural rights indispensable for his dignity and the free development of his personality.

Article 23

(1) Everyone has the right to work, to free choice of employment, to just and favourable conditions of work and to protection against unemployment.

(2) Everyone, without any discrimination, has the right to equal pay for equal work.

(3) Everyone who works has the right to just and favourable remuneration ensuring for himself and his family an existence worthy of human dignity, and supplemented, if necessary, by other means of social protection.

(4) Everyone has the right to form and to join trade unions for the protection of his interests.

Article 24

Everyone has the right to rest and leisure, including reasonable limitation of working hours and periodic holidays with pay.

Article 25

(1) Everyone has the right to a standard of living adequate for the health and well-being of himself and of his family, including food, clothing, housing and medical care and necessary social services, and the right to security in the event of unemployment, sickness, disability, widowhood, old age or other lack of livelihood in circumstances beyond his control.

(2) Motherhood and childhood are entitled to special care and assistance. All children, whether born in or out of wedlock, shall enjoy the same social protection.

Article 26

(1) Everyone has the right to education. Education shall be free, at least in the elementary and fundamental stages. Elementary education shall be compulsory. Technical and professional education shall be made generally available and higher education shall be equally accessible to all on the basis of merit.

(2) Education shall be directed to the full development of the human personality and to the strengthening of respect for human rights and fundamental freedoms. It shall promote understanding, tolerance and friendship among all nations, racial or religious groups, and shall further the activities of the United Nations for the maintenance of peace.

(3) Parents have a prior right to choose the kind of education that shall be given to their children.

Article 27

(1) Everyone has the right freely to participate in the cultural life of the community, to enjoy the arts and to share in scientific advancement and its benefits.

(2) Everyone has the right to the protection of the moral and material interests resulting from any scientific, literary or artistic production of which he is the author.

Article 28

Everyone is entitled to a social and international order in which the rights and freedoms set forth in this Declaration can be fully realized.

Article 29

(1) Everyone has duties to the community in which alone the free and full development of his personality is possible.

(2) In the exercise of his rights and freedoms, everyone shall be subject only to such limitations as are determined by law solely for the purpose of securing due recognition and respect for the rights and freedoms of others and of meeting the just requirements of morality, public order and the general welfare in a democratic society.

(3) These rights and freedoms may in no case be exercised contrary to the purposes and principles of the United Nations.

Article 30

Nothing in this Declaration may be interpreted as implying for any State, group or person any right to engage in any activity or to perform any act aimed at the destruction of any of the rights and freedoms set forth herein.

Data till November 3, 2008

* Data till November 3, 2008

APPENDIX V

INTERNATIONAL COVENANT ON CIVIL AND POLITICAL RIGHTS

Adopted and opened for signature, ratification and accession by General Assembly resolution 2200A (XXI)of 16 December 1966 entry into force 23 March 1976, in accordance with Article 49

Preamble

The States Parties to the present Covenant,

Considering that, in accordance with the principles proclaimed in the Charter of the United Nations, recognition of the inherent dignity and of the equal and inalienable rights of all members of the human family is the foundation of freedom, justice and peace in the world,

Recognizing that these rights derive from the inherent dignity of the human person,

Recognizing that, in accordance with the Universal Declaration of Human Rights, the ideal of free human beings enjoying civil and political freedom and freedom from fear and want can only be achieved if conditions are created whereby everyone may enjoy his civil and political rights, as well as his economic, social and cultural rights,

Considering the obligation of States under the Charter of the United Nations to promote universal respect for, and observance of, human rights and freedoms,

Realizing that the individual, having duties to other individuals and to the community to which he belongs, is under a responsibility to strive for the promotion and observance of the rights recognized in the present Covenant,

Agree upon the following articles:

PART I

Article 1

1. All peoples have the right of self-determination. By virtue of that right they freely determine their political status and freely pursue their economic, social and cultural development.

2. All peoples may, for their own ends, freely dispose of their natural wealth and resources without prejudice to any obligations arising out of international economic co-operation, based upon the principle of mutual benefit, and international law. In no case may a people be deprived of its own means of subsistence.

3. The States Parties to the present Covenant, including those having responsibility for the administration of Non-Self-Governing and Trust Territories, shall promote the realization of the right of self-determination, and shall respect that right, in conformity with the provisions of the Charter of the United Nations.

PART II

Article 2

1. Each State Party to the present Covenant undertakes to respect and to ensure to all individuals within its territory and subject to its jurisdiction the rights recognized in the present Covenant, without distinction of any kind, such as race, colour, sex, language, religion, political or other opinion, national or social origin, property, birth or other status.

2. Where not already provided for by existing legislative or other measures, each State Party to the present Covenant undertakes to take the necessary steps, in accordance with its constitutional processes and with the provisions of the present Covenant, to adopt such laws or other measures as may be necessary to give effect to the rights recognized in the present Covenant.

3. Each State Party to the present Covenant undertakes:

   (a) To ensure that any person whose rights or freedoms as herein recognized are violated shall have an effective remedy, notwithstanding that the violation has been committed by persons acting in an official capacity;

   (b) To ensure that any person claiming such a remedy shall have his right thereto determined by competent judicial, administrative or legislative authorities, or by any other competent authority provided for by the legal system of the State, and to develop the possibilities of judicial remedy;

(c) To ensure that the competent authorities shall enforce such remedies when granted.

Article 3

The States Parties to the present Covenant undertake to ensure the equal right of men and women to the enjoyment of all civil and political rights set forth in the present Covenant.

Article 4

1. In time of public emergency which threatens the life of the nation and the existence of which is officially proclaimed, the States Parties to the present Covenant may take measures derogating from their obligations under the present Covenant to the extent strictly required by the exigencies of the situation, provided that such measures are not inconsistent with their other obligations under international law and do not involve discrimination solely on the ground of race, colour, sex, language, religion or social origin.

2. No derogation from articles 6, 7, 8 (paragraphs I and 2), 11, 15, 16 and 18 may be made under this provision.

3. Any State Party to the present Covenant availing itself of the right of derogation shall immediately inform the other States Parties to the present Covenant, through the intermediary of the Secretary-General of the United Nations, of the provisions from which it has derogated and of the reasons by which it was actuated. A further communication shall be made, through the same intermediary, on the date on which it terminates such derogation.

Article 5

1. Nothing in the present Covenant may be interpreted as implying for any State, group or person any right to engage in any activity or perform any act aimed at the destruction of any of the rights and freedoms recognized herein or at their limitation to a greater extent than is provided for in the present Covenant.

2. There shall be no restriction upon or derogation from any of

the fundamental human rights recognized or existing in any State Party to the present Covenant pursuant to law, conventions, regulations or custom on the pretext that the present Covenant does not recognize such rights or that it recognizes them to a lesser extent.

PART III

Article 6

1. Every human being has the inherent right to life. This right shall be protected by law. No one shall be arbitrarily deprived of his life.
2. In countries which have not abolished the death penalty, sentence of death may be imposed only for the most serious crimes in accordance with the law in force at the time of the commission of the crime and not contrary to the provisions of the present Covenant and to the Convention on the Prevention and Punishment of the Crime of Genocide. This penalty can only be carried out pursuant to a final judgement rendered by a competent court.
3. When deprivation of life constitutes the crime of genocide, it is understood that nothing in this article shall authorize any State Party to the present Covenant to derogate in any way from any obligation assumed under the provisions of the Convention on the Prevention and Punishment of the Crime of Genocide.
4. Anyone sentenced to death shall have the right to seek pardon or commutation of the sentence. Amnesty, pardon or commutation of the sentence of death may be granted in all cases.
5. Sentence of death shall not be imposed for crimes committed by persons below eighteen years of age and shall not be carried out on pregnant women.
6. Nothing in this article shall be invoked to delay or to prevent the abolition of capital punishment by any State Party to the present Covenant.

Article 7

No one shall be subjected to torture or to cruel, inhuman or degrading treatment or punishment. In particular, no one shall be subjected without his free consent to medical or scientific experimentation.

Article 8

1. No one shall be held in slavery; slavery and the slave-trade in all their forms shall be prohibited.

2. No one shall be held in servitude.

3.(a) No one shall be required to perform forced or compulsory labour;

(b) Paragraph 3 (a) shall not be held to preclude, in countries where imprisonment with hard labour may be imposed as a punishment for a crime, the performance of hard labour in pursuance of a sentence to such punishment by a competent court;

(c) For the purpose of this paragraph the term "forced or compulsory labour" shall not include:

(i) Any work or service, not referred to in subparagraph

(b), normally required of a person who is under detention in consequence of a lawful order of a court, or of a person during conditional release from such detention;

(ii) Any service of a military character and, in countries where conscientious objection is recognized, any national service required by law of conscientious objectors;

(iii) Any service exacted in cases of emergency or calamity threatening the life or well-being of the community;

(iv) Any work or service which forms part of normal civil obligations.

Article 9

1. Everyone has the right to liberty and security of person. No one shall be subjected to arbitrary arrest or detention. No one shall be deprived of his liberty except on such grounds and in accordance with such procedure as are established by law.

2. Anyone who is arrested shall be informed, at the time of arrest, of the reasons for his arrest and shall be promptly informed of any charges against him.

3. Anyone arrested or detained on a criminal charge shall be brought promptly before a judge or other officer authorized by law to exercise judicial power and shall be entitled to trial within a reasonable time or to release. It shall not be the general rule that persons awaiting trial shall be detained in custody, but release may be subject to guarantees to appear for trial, at any other stage of the judicial proceedings, and, should occasion arise, for execution of the judgement.

4. Anyone who is deprived of his liberty by arrest or detention shall be entitled to take proceedings before a court, in order that that court may decide without delay on the lawfulness of his detention and order his release if the detention is not lawful.

5. Anyone who has been the victim of unlawful arrest or detention shall have an enforceable right to compensation.

Article 10

1. All persons deprived of their liberty shall be treated with humanity and with respect for the inherent dignity of the human person.

2. (a) Accused persons shall, save in exceptional circumstances, be segregated from convicted persons and shall be subject to separate treatment appropriate to their status as unconvicted persons;

(b) Accused juvenile persons shall be separated from adults and brought as speedily as possible for adjudication.

3. The penitentiary system shall comprise treatment of prisoners the essential aim of which shall be their reformation and social rehabilitation. Juvenile offenders shall be segregated from adults and be accorded treatment appropriate to their age and legal status.

Article 11

No one shall be imprisoned merely on the ground of inability to fulfil a contractual obligation.

Article 12

1. Everyone lawfully within the territory of a State shall, within that territory, have the right to liberty of movement and freedom to choose his residence.

2. Everyone shall be free to leave any country, including his own.

3. The above-mentioned rights shall not be subject to any restrictions except those which are provided by law, are necessary to protect national security, public order (ordre public), public health or morals or the rights and freedoms of others, and are consistent with the other rights recognized in the present Covenant.

4. No one shall be arbitrarily deprived of the right to enter his own country.

Article 13

An alien lawfully in the territory of a State Party to the present Covenant may be expelled therefrom only in pursuance of a decision reached in accordance with law and shall, except where compelling reasons of national security otherwise require, be allowed to submit the reasons against his expulsion and to have his case reviewed by, and be represented for the purpose before, the competent authority or a person or persons especially designated by the competent authority.

Article 14

1. All persons shall be equal before the courts and tribunals. In the determination of any criminal charge against him, or of his rights and obligations in a suit at law, everyone shall be entitled to a fair and public hearing by a competent, independent and impartial tribunal established by law. The press and the public may be excluded from all or part of a trial for reasons of morals, public order (ordre public) or national security in a democratic society, or when the interest of the private lives of the parties so requires, or to the extent strictly necessary in the opinion of the court in special circumstances where publicity would prejudice the interests of justice; but any judgement rendered in a criminal case or in a suit at law shall be made public except where the

interest of juvenile persons otherwise requires or the proceedings concern matrimonial disputes or the guardianship of children. 2. Everyone charged with a criminal offence shall have the right to be presumed innocent until proved guilty according to law. 3. In the determination of any criminal charge against him, everyone shall be entitled to the following minimum guarantees, in full equality:

(a) To be informed promptly and in detail in a language which he understands of the nature and cause of the charge against him;

(b) To have adequate time and facilities for the preparation of his defence and to communicate with counsel of his own choosing;

(c) To be tried without undue delay;

(d) To be tried in his presence, and to defend himself in person or through legal assistance of his own choosing; to be informed, if he does not have legal assistance, of this right; and to have legal assistance assigned to him, in any case where the interests of justice so require, and without payment by him in any such case if he does not have sufficient means to pay for it;

(e) To examine, or have examined, the witnesses against him and to obtain the attendance and examination of witnesses on his behalf under the same conditions as witnesses against him;

(f) To have the free assistance of an interpreter if he cannot understand or speak the language used in court;

(g) Not to be compelled to testify against himself or to confess guilt. 4. In the case of juvenile persons, the procedure shall be such as will take account of their age and the desirability of promoting their rehabilitation.

5. Everyone convicted of a crime shall have the right to his conviction and sentence being reviewed by a higher tribunal according to law.

6. When a person has by a final decision been convicted of a

criminal offence and when subsequently his conviction has been reversed or he has been pardoned on the ground that a new or newly discovered fact shows conclusively that there has been a miscarriage of justice, the person who has suffered punishment as a result of such conviction shall be compensated according to law, unless it is proved that the non-disclosure of the unknown fact in time is wholly or partly attributable to him.

7. No one shall be liable to be tried or punished again for an offence for which he has already been finally convicted or acquitted in accordance with the law and penal procedure of each country.

Article 15

1. No one shall be held guilty of any criminal offence on account of any act or omission which did not constitute a criminal offence, under national or international law, at the time when it was committed. Nor shall a heavier penalty be imposed than the one that was applicable at the time when the criminal offence was committed. If, subsequent to the commission of the offence, provision is made by law for the imposition of the lighter penalty, the offender shall benefit thereby.
2. Nothing in this article shall prejudice the trial and punishment of any person for any act or omission which, at the time when it was committed, was criminal according to the general principles of law recognized by the community of nations.

Article 16

Everyone shall have the right to recognition everywhere as a person before the law.

Article 17

1. No one shall be subjected to arbitrary or unlawful interference with his privacy, family, home or correspondence, nor to unlawful attacks on his honour and reputation.
2. Everyone has the right to the protection of the law against such interference or attacks.

Article 18

1. Everyone shall have the right to freedom of thought, conscience and religion. This right shall include freedom to have or to adopt a religion or belief of his choice, and freedom, either individually or in community with others and in public or private, to manifest his religion or belief in worship, observance, practice and teaching. 2. No one shall be subject to coercion which would impair his freedom to have or to adopt a religion or belief of his choice. 3. Freedom to manifest one's religion or beliefs may be subject only to such limitations as are prescribed by law and are necessary to protect public safety, order, health, or morals or the fundamental rights and freedoms of others. 4. The States Parties to the present Covenant undertake to have respect for the liberty of parents and, when applicable, legal guardians to ensure the religious and moral education of their children in conformity with their own convictions.

Article 19

1. Everyone shall have the right to hold opinions without interference.
2. Everyone shall have the right to freedom of expression; this right shall include freedom to seek, receive and impart information and ideas of all kinds, regardless of frontiers, either orally, in writing or in print, in the form of art, or through any other media of his choice.
3. The exercise of the rights provided for in paragraph 2 of this article carries with it special duties and responsibilities. It may therefore be subject to certain restrictions, but these shall only be such as are provided by law and are necessary:

    (a) For respect of the rights or reputations of others;

    (b) For the protection of national security or of public order (ordre publi

    c), or of public health or morals.

Article 20

1. Any propaganda for war shall be prohibited by law. 2. Any advocacy of national, racial or religious hatred that constitutes

incitement to discrimination, hostility or violence shall be prohibited by law.

Article 21

The right of peaceful assembly shall be recognized. No restrictions may be placed on the exercise of this right other than those imposed in conformity with the law and which are necessary in a democratic society in the interests of national security or public safety, public order (ordre public), the protection of public health or morals or the protection of the rights and freedoms of others.

Article 22

1. Everyone shall have the right to freedom of association with others, including the right to form and join trade unions for the protection of his interests.
2. No restrictions may be placed on the exercise of this right other than those which are prescribed by law and which are necessary in a democratic society in the interests of national security or public safety, public order (ordre public), the protection of public health or morals or the protection of the rights and freedoms of others. This article shall not prevent the imposition of lawful restrictions on members of the armed forces and of the police in their exercise of this right.
3. Nothing in this article shall authorize States Parties to the International Labour Organisation Convention of 1948 concerning Freedom of Association and Protection of the Right to Organize to take legislative measures which would prejudice, or to apply the law in such a manner as to prejudice, the guarantees provided for in that Convention.

Article 23

1. The family is the natural and fundamental group unit of society and is entitled to protection by society and the State.
2. The right of men and women of marriageable age to marry and to found a family shall be recognized.
3. No marriage shall be entered into without the free and full consent of the intending spouses.

4. States Parties to the present Covenant shall take appropriate steps to ensure equality of rights and responsibilities of spouses as to marriage, during marriage and at its dissolution. In the case of dissolution, provision shall be made for the necessary protection of any children.

Article 24

1. Every child shall have, without any discrimination as to race, colour, sex, language, religion, national or social origin, property or birth, the right to such measures of protection as are required by his status as a minor, on the part of his family, society and the State.
2. Every child shall be registered immediately after birth and shall have a name.
3. Every child has the right to acquire a nationality.

Article 25

Every citizen shall have the right and the opportunity, without any of the distinctions mentioned in article 2 and without unreasonable restrictions:

(a) To take part in the conduct of public affairs, directly or through freely chosen representatives;

(b) To vote and to be elected at genuine periodic elections which shall be by universal and equal suffrage and shall be held by secret ballot, guaranteeing the free expression of the will of the electors;

(c) To have access, on general terms of equality, to public service in his country.

Article 26

All persons are equal before the law and are entitled without any discrimination to the equal protection of the law. In this respect, the law shall prohibit any discrimination and guarantee to all persons equal and effective protection against discrimination on any ground such as race, colour, sex, language, religion, political or other opinion, national or social origin, property, birth or other status.

Article 27

In those States in which ethnic, religious or linguistic minorities exist, persons belonging to such minorities shall not be denied the right, in community with the other members of their group, to enjoy their own culture, to profess and practise their own religion, or to use their own language.

PART IV

Article 28

1. There shall be established a Human Rights Committee (hereafter referred to in the present Covenant as the Committee). It shall consist of eighteen members and shall carry out the functions hereinafter provided.
2. The Committee shall be composed of nationals of the States Parties to the present Covenant who shall be persons of high moral character and recognized competence in the field of human rights, consideration being given to the usefulness of the participation of some persons having legal experience.
3. The members of the Committee shall be elected and shall serve in their personal capacity.

Article 29

1. The members of the Committee shall be elected by secret ballot from a list of persons possessing the qualifications prescribed in article 28 and nominated for the purpose by the States Parties to the present Covenant.
2. Each State Party to the present Covenant may nominate not more than two persons. These persons shall be nationals of the nominating State.
3. A person shall be eligible for renomination.

Article 30

1. The initial election shall be held no later than six months after the date of the entry into force of the present Covenant.
2. At least four months before the date of each election to the Committee, other than an election to fill a vacancy declared in accordance with article 34, the Secretary-General of the

United Nations shall address a written invitation to the States Parties to the present Covenant to submit their nominations for membership of the Committee within three months.

3. The Secretary-General of the United Nations shall prepare a list in alphabetical order of all the persons thus nominated, with an indication of the States Parties which have nominated them, and shall submit it to the States Parties to the present Covenant no later than one month before the date of each election.

4. Elections of the members of the Committee shall be held at a meeting of the States Parties to the present Covenant convened by the Secretary General of the United Nations at the Headquarters of the United Nations. At that meeting, for which two thirds of the States Parties to the present Covenant shall constitute a quorum, the persons elected to the Committee shall be those nominees who obtain the largest number of votes and an absolute majority of the votes of the representatives of States Parties present and voting.

Article 31

1. The Committee may not include more than one national of the same State.

2. In the election of the Committee, consideration shall be given to equitable geographical distribution of membership and to the representation of the different forms of civilization and of the principal legal systems.

Article 32

1. The members of the Committee shall be elected for a term of four years. They shall be eligible for re-election if renominated. However, the terms of nine of the members elected at the first election shall expire at the end of two years; immediately after the first election, the names of these nine members shall be chosen by lot by the Chairman of the meeting referred to in article 30, paragraph 4.

2. Elections at the expiry of office shall be held in accordance with the preceding articles of this part of the present Covenant.

Article 33

1. If, in the unanimous opinion of the other members, a member of the Committee has ceased to carry out his functions for any cause other than absence of a temporary character, the Chairman of the Committee shall notify the Secretary-General of the United Nations, who shall then declare the seat of that member to be vacant.
2. In the event of the death or the resignation of a member of the Committee, the Chairman shall immediately notify the Secretary-General of the United Nations, who shall declare the seat vacant from the date of death or the date on which the resignation takes effect.

Article 34

1. When a vacancy is declared in accordance with article 33 and if the term of office of the member to be replaced does not expire within six months of the declaration of the vacancy, the Secretary-General of the United Nations shall notify each of the States Parties to the present Covenant, which may within two months submit nominations in accordance with article 29 for the purpose of filling the vacancy.
2. The Secretary-General of the United Nations shall prepare a list in alphabetical order of the persons thus nominated and shall submit it to the States Parties to the present Covenant. The election to fill the vacancy shall then take place in accordance with the relevant provisions of this part of the present Covenant.
3. A member of the Committee elected to fill a vacancy declared in accordance with article 33 shall hold office for the remainder of the term of the member who vacated the seat on the Committee under the provisions of that article.

Article 35

The members of the Committee shall, with the approval of the General Assembly of the United Nations, receive emoluments from United Nations resources on such terms and conditions as the General Assembly may decide, having regard to the importance of the Committee's responsibilities.

Article 36

The Secretary-General of the United Nations shall provide the necessary staff and facilities for the effective performance of the functions of the Committee under the present Covenant.

Article 37

1. The Secretary-General of the United Nations shall convene the initial meeting of the Committee at the Headquarters of the United Nations.
2. After its initial meeting, the Committee shall meet at such times as shall be provided in its rules of procedure.
3. The Committee shall normally meet at the Headquarters of the United Nations or at the United Nations Office at Geneva.

Article 38

Every member of the Committee shall, before taking up his duties, make a solemn declaration in open committee that he will perform his functions impartially and conscientiously.

Article 39

1. The Committee shall elect its officers for a term of two years. They may be re-elected.
2. The Committee shall establish its own rules of procedure, but these rules shall provide, inter alia, that:

(a) Twelve members shall constitute a quorum;

(b) Decisions of the Committee shall be made by a majority vote of the members present.

Article 40

1. The States Parties to the present Covenant undertake to submit reports on the measures they have adopted which give effect to the rights recognized herein and on the progress made in the enjoyment of those rights:

   (a) Within one year of the entry into force of the present Covenant for the States Parties concerned;

   (b) Thereafter whenever the Committee so requests.

2. All reports shall be submitted to the Secretary-General of the United Nations, who shall transmit them to the Committee for consideration. Reports shall indicate the factors and difficulties, if any, affecting the implementation of the present Covenant.
3. The Secretary-General of the United Nations may, after consultation with the Committee, transmit to the specialized agencies concerned copies of such parts of the reports as may fall within their field of competence.
4. The Committee shall study the reports submitted by the States Parties to the present Covenant. It shall transmit its reports, and such general comments as it may consider appropriate, to the States Parties. The Committee may also transmit to the Economic and Social Council these comments along with the copies of the reports it has received from States Parties to the present Covenant.
5. The States Parties to the present Covenant may submit to the Committee observations on any comments that may be made in accordance with paragraph 4 of this article.

Article 41

1. A State Party to the present Covenant may at any time declare under this article that it recognizes the competence of the Committee to receive and consider communications to the effect that a State Party claims that another State Party is not fulfilling its obligations under the present Covenant. Communications under this article may be received and considered only if submitted by a State Party which has made a declaration recognizing in regard to itself the competence of the Committee. No communication shall be received by the Committee if it concerns a State Party which has not made such a declaration. Communications received under this article shall be dealt with in accordance with the following procedure:

(a) If a State Party to the present Covenant considers that another State Party is not giving effect to the provisions of the present Covenant, it may, by written communication, bring the matter to the attention of that State Party. Within three months after the receipt of the communication the receiving State shall afford the State which sent the communication an explanation, or any other statement in writing clarifying the matter which should include, to the extent possible and pertinent, reference to domestic procedures and remedies taken, pending, or available in the matter;

(b) If the matter is not adjusted to the satisfaction of both States Parties concerned within six months after the receipt by the receiving State of the initial communication, either State shall have the right to refer the matter to the Committee, by notice given to the Committee and to the other State;

(c) The Committee shall deal with a matter referred to it only after it has ascertained that all available domestic remedies have been invoked and exhausted in the matter, in conformity with the generally recognized principles of international law. This shall not be the rule where the application of the remedies is unreasonably prolonged;

(d) The Committee shall hold closed meetings when examining communications under this article;

(e) Subject to the provisions of subparagraph (c), the Committee shall make available its good offices to the States Parties concerned with a view to a friendly solution of the matter on the basis of respect for human rights and fundamental freedoms as recognized in the present Covenant;

(f) In any matter referred to it, the Committee may call upon the States Parties concerned, referred to in subparagraph (b), to supply any relevant information;

(g) The States Parties concerned, referred to in subparagraph (b), shall have the right to be represented when the matter is being considered in the Committee and to make submissions orally and/or in writing;

(h) The Committee shall, within twelve months after the date of receipt of notice under subparagraph (b), submit a report:

(i) If a solution within the terms of subparagraph (e) is

reached, the Committee shall confine its report to a brief statement of the facts and of the solution reached;

(ii) If a solution within the terms of subparagraph (e) is not reached, the Committee shall confine its report to a brief statement of the facts; the written submissions and record of the oral submissions made by the States Parties concerned shall be attached to the report. In every matter, the report shall be communicated to the States Parties concerned.

2. The provisions of this article shall come into force when ten States Parties to the present Covenant have made declarations under paragraph I of this article. Such declarations shall be deposited by the States Parties with the Secretary-General of the United Nations, who shall transmit copies thereof to the other States Parties. A declaration may be withdrawn at any time by notification to the Secretary-General. Such a withdrawal shall not prejudice the consideration of any matter which is the subject of a communication already transmitted under this article; no further communication by any State Party shall be received after the notification of withdrawal of the declaration has been received by the Secretary-General, unless the State Party concerned has made a new declaration.

Article 42

1. (a) If a matter referred to the Committee in accordance with article 41 is not resolved to the satisfaction of the States Parties concerned, the Committee may, with the prior consent of the States Parties concerned, appoint an ad hoc Conciliation Commission (hereinafter referred to as the Commission). The good offices of the Commission shall be made available to the States Parties concerned with a view to an amicable solution of the matter on the basis of respect for the present Covenant;

(b) The Commission shall consist of five persons acceptable to the States Parties concerned. If the States Parties concerned fail to reach agreement within three months on all or part of the composition of the Commission, the members of the Commission concerning whom no agreement has been reached shall be elected by secret ballot by a two-thirds majority vote of the Committee from among its members. 2. The members of the Commission shall serve in their personal capacity. They shall not be nationals of the States Parties concerned, or of a State not Party to the present Covenant, or of a State Party which has not made a declaration under article 41.3. The Commission shall elect its own Chairman and adopt its own rules of procedure.

4. The meetings of the Commission shall normally be held at the Headquarters of the United Nations or at the United Nations Office at Geneva. However, they may be held at such other convenient places as the Commission may determine in consultation with the Secretary-General of the United Nations and the States Parties concerned.

5. The secretariat provided in accordance with article 36 shall also service the commissions appointed under this article.

6. The information received and collated by the Committee shall be made available to the Commission and the Commission may call upon the States Parties concerned to supply any other relevant information.

7. When the Commission has fully considered the matter, but in any event not later than twelve months after having been seized of the matter, it shall submit to the Chairman of the Committee a report for communication to the States Parties concerned:

(a) If the Commission is unable to complete its consideration of the matter within twelve months, it shall confine its report to a brief statement of the status of its consideration of the matter;

(b) If an amicable solution to the matter on tie basis of respect for human rights as recognized in the present Covenant is reached, the Commission shall confinc its report to a brief statement of the facts and of the solution reached; (c) If a solution within the terms of subparagraph (b) is not reached, the Commission's report shall embody its findings on all questions of fact relevant to the issues between the States Parties concerned, and its views on the possibilities of an amicable solution of the matter. This report shall also contain the written submissions and a record of the oral submissions made by the States Parties concerned; (d) If the Commission's report is submitted under subparagraph (c), the States Parties concerned shall, within three months of the receipt of the report, notify the Chairman of the Committee whether or not they accept the contents of the report of the Commission. 8. The provisions of this article are without prejudice to the responsibilities of the Committee under article 41. 9. The States Parties concerned shall share equally all the expenses of the members of the Commission in accordance with estimates to be provided by the Secretary-General of the United Nations. 10. The Secretary-General of the United Nations shall be empowered to pay the expenses of the members of the Commission, if necessary, before reimbursement by the States Parties concerned, in accordance with paragraph 9 of this article.

Article 43

The members of the Committee, and of the ad hoc conciliation commissions which may be appointed under article 42, shall be entitled to the facilities, privileges and immunities of experts on mission for the United Nations as laid down in the relevant sections of the Convention on the Privileges and Immunities of the United Nations.

Article 44

The provisions for the implementation of the present Covenant shall apply without prejudice to the procedures prescribed in the field of human rights by or under the constituent instruments and the conventions of the United Nations and of the specialized agencies and shall not prevent the States Parties to the present Covenant from having recourse to other procedures for settling a dispute in accordance with general or special international agreements in force between them.

Article 45

The Committee shall submit to the General Assembly of the United Nations, through the Economic and Social Council, an annual report on its activities.

PART V

Article 46

Nothing in the present Covenant shall be interpreted as impairing the provisions of the Charter of the United Nations and of the constitutions of the specialized agencies which define the respective responsibilities of the various organs of the United Nations and of the specialized agencies in regard to the matters dealt with in the present Covenant.

Article 47

Nothing in the present Covenant shall be interpreted as impairing the inherent right of all peoples to enjoy and utilize fully and freely their natural wealth and resources.

PART VI

Article 48

1. The present Covenant is open for signature by any State Member of the United Nations or member of any of its specialized agencies, by any State Party to the Statute of the International Court of Justice, and by any other State which has been invited by the General Assembly of the United Nations to become a Party to the present Covenant.
2. The present Covenant is subject to ratification. Instruments of ratification shall be deposited with the Secretary-General of the United Nations.
3. The present Covenant shall be open to accession by any State referred to in paragraph 1 of this article.
4. Accession shall be effected by the deposit of an instrument of accession with the Secretary-General of the United Nations.
5. The Secretary-General of the United Nations shall inform all States which have signed this Covenant or acceded to it of the deposit of each instrument of ratification or accession.

Article 49

1. The present Covenant shall enter into force three months after the date of the deposit with the Secretary-General of the

United Nations of the thirty-fifth instrument of ratification or instrument of accession.

2. For each State ratifying the present Covenant or acceding to it after the deposit of the thirty-fifth instrument of ratification or instrument of accession, the present Covenant shall enter into force three months after the date of the deposit of its own instrument of ratification or instrument of accession.

Article 50

The provisions of the present Covenant shall extend to all parts of federal States without any limitations or exceptions.

Article 51

1. Any State Party to the present Covenant may propose an amendment and file it with the Secretary-General of the United Nations. The Secretary-General of the United Nations shall thereupon communicate any proposed amendments to the States Parties to the present Covenant with a request that they notify him whether they favour a conference of States Parties for the purpose of considering and voting upon the proposals. In the event that at least one third of the States Parties favours such a conference, the Secretary-General shall convene the conference under the auspices of the United Nations. Any amendment adopted by a majority of the States Parties present and voting at the conference shall be submitted to the General Assembly of the United Nations for approval.

2. Amendments shall come into force when they have been approved by the General Assembly of the United Nations and accepted by a two-thirds majority of the States Parties to the present Covenant in accordance with their respective constitutional processes.

3. When amendments come into force, they shall be binding on those States Parties which have accepted them, other States Parties still being bound by the provisions of the present Covenant and any earlier amendment which they have accepted.

Article 52

1. Irrespective of the notifications made under article 48, paragraph 5, the Secretary-General of the United Nations shall inform all States referred to in paragraph I of the same article of the following particulars:

(a) Signatures, ratifications and accessions under article 48;

(b) The date of the entry into force of the present Covenant under article 49 and the date of the entry into force of any amendments under article 51.

Article 53

1. The present Covenant, of which the Chinese, English, French, Russian and Spanish texts are equally authentic, shall be deposited in the archives of the United Nations.

2. The Secretary-General of the United Nations shall transmit certified copies of the present Covenant to all States referred to in article 48.

APPENDIX VI
INTERNATIONAL COVENANT ON ECONOMIC, SOCIAL AND CULTURAL RIGHTS

Adopted and opened for signature, ratification and accession by General Assembly resolution 2200A (XXI) of 16 December 1966 entry into force 3 January 1976, in accordance with article 27

Preamble

The States Parties to the present Covenant,

Considering that, in accordance with the principles proclaimed in the Charter of the United Nations, recognition of the inherent dignity and of the equal and inalienable rights of all members of the human family is the foundation of freedom, justice and peace in the world,

Recognizing that these rights derive from the inherent dignity of the human person,

Recognizing that, in accordance with the Universal Declaration of Human Rights, the ideal of free human beings enjoying freedom from fear and want can only be achieved if conditions are created whereby everyone may enjoy his economic, social and cultural rights, as well as his civil and political rights,

Considering the obligation of States under the Charter of the United Nations to promote universal respect for, and observance of, human rights and freedoms,

Realizing that the individual, having duties to other individuals and to the community to which he belongs, is under a responsibility to strive for the promotion and observance of the rights recognized in the present Covenant,

Agree upon the following articles:

PART I

Article 1

1. All peoples have the right of self-determination. By virtue of that right they freely determine their political status and freely pursue their economic, social and cultural development.

2. All peoples may, for their own ends, freely dispose of their natural wealth and resources without prejudice to any obligations arising out of international economic co-operation, based upon the principle of mutual benefit, and international law. In no case may a people be deprived of its own means of subsistence.
3. The States Parties to the present Covenant, including those having responsibility for the administration of Non-Self-Governing and Trust Territories, shall promote the realization of the right of self-determination, and shall respect that right, in conformity with the provisions of the Charter of the United Nations.

PART II

Article 2

1. Each State Party to the present Covenant undertakes to take steps, individually and through international assistance and co-operation, especially economic and technical, to the maximum of its available resources, with a view to achieving progressively the full realization of the rights recognized in the present Covenant by all appropriate means, including particularly the adoption of legislative measures.
2. The States Parties to the present Covenant undertake to guarantee that the rights enunciated in the present Covenant will be exercised without discrimination of any kind as to race, colour, sex, language, religion, political or other opinion, national or social origin, property, birth or other status.
3. Developing countries, with due regard to human rights and their national economy, may determine to what extent they would guarantee the economic rights recognized in the present Covenant to non-nationals.

Article 3

The States Parties to the present Covenant undertake to ensure the equal right of men and women to the enjoyment of all economic, social and cultural rights set forth in the present Covenant.

Article 4

The States Parties to the present Covenant recognize that, in the enjoyment of those rights provided by the State in conformity with the present Covenant, the State may subject such rights only to such limitations as are determined by law only in so far as this may be compatible with the nature of these rights and solely for the purpose of promoting the general welfare in a democratic society.

Article 5

1. Nothing in the present Covenant may be interpreted as implying for any State, group or person any right to engage in any activity or to perform any act aimed at the destruction of any of the rights or freedoms recognized herein, or at their limitation to a greater extent than is provided for in the present Covenant.

2. No restriction upon or derogation from any of the fundamental human rights recognized or existing in any country in virtue of law, conventions, regulations or custom shall be admitted on the pretext that the present Covenant does not recognize such rights or that it recognizes them to a lesser extent.

PART III

Article 6

1. The States Parties to the present Covenant recognize the right to work, which includes the right of everyone to the opportunity to gain his living by work which he freely chooses or accepts, and will take appropriate steps to safeguard this right.

2. The steps to be taken by a State Party to the present Covenant to achieve the full realization of this right shall include technical and vocational guidance and training programmes, policies and techniques to achieve steady economic, social and cultural development and full and productive employment under conditions safeguarding fundamental political and economic freedoms to the individual.

Article 7

The States Parties to the present Covenant recognize the

right of everyone to the enjoyment of just and favourable conditions of work which ensure, in particular:

(a) Remuneration which provides all workers, as a minimum, with:

  (i) Fair wages and equal remuneration for work of equal value without distinction of any kind, in particular women being guaranteed conditions of work not inferior to those enjoyed by men, with equal pay for equal work;

  (ii) A decent living for themselves and their families in accordance with the provisions of the present Covenant;

(b) Safe and healthy working conditions;

(c) Equal opportunity for everyone to be promoted in his employment to an appropriate higher level, subject to no considerations other than those of seniority and competence;

(d) Rest, leisure and reasonable limitation of working hours and periodic holidays with pay, as well as remuneration for public holidays

Article 8

1. The States Parties to the present Covenant undertake to ensure:

   (a) The right of everyone to form trade unions and join the trade union of his choice, subject only to the rules of the organization concerned, for the promotion and protection of his economic and social interests. No restrictions may be placed on the exercise of this right other than those prescribed by law and which are necessary in a democratic society in the interests of national security or public order or for the protection of the rights and freedoms of others;

   (b) The right of trade unions to establish national federations or confederations and the right of the latter to form or join international trade-union organizations;

   (c) The right of trade unions to function freely subject to no limitations other than those prescribed by law and which are necessary in a democratic society in the interests of national security or public order or for the protection of the rights and freedoms of others;

(d) The right to strike, provided that it is exercised in conformity with the laws of the particular country.

2. This article shall not prevent the imposition of lawful restrictions on the exercise of these rights by members of the armed forces or of the police or of the administration of the State.

3. Nothing in this article shall authorize States Parties to the International Labour Organisation Convention of 1948 concerning Freedom of Association and Protection of the Right to Organize to take legislative measures which would prejudice, or apply the law in such a manner as would prejudice, the guarantees provided for in that Convention.

Article 9

The States Parties to the present Covenant recognize the right of everyone to social security, including social insurance.

Article 10

The States Parties to the present Covenant recognize that:

1. The widest possible protection and assistance should be accorded to the family, which is the natural and fundamental group unit of society, particularly for its establishment and while it is responsible for the care and education of dependent children. Marriage must be entered into with the free consent of the intending spouses.

2. Special protection should be accorded to mothers during a reasonable period before and after childbirth. During such period working mothers should be accorded paid leave or leave with adequate social security benefits.

3. Special measures of protection and assistance should be taken on behalf of all children and young persons without any discrimination for reasons of parentage or other conditions. Children and young persons should be protected from economic and social exploitation. Their employment in work harmful

to their morals or health or dangerous to life or likely to hamper their normal development should be punishable by law. States should also set age limits below which the paid employment of child labour should be prohibited and punishable by law.

Article 11

1. The States Parties to the present Covenant recognize the right of everyone to an adequate standard of living for himself and his family, including adequate food, clothing and housing, and to the continuous improvement of living conditions. The States Parties will take appropriate steps to ensure the realization of this right, recognizing to this effect the essential importance of international co-operation based on free consent.

2. The States Parties to the present Covenant, recognizing the fundamental right of everyone to be free from hunger, shall take, individually and through international co-operation, the measures, including specific programmes, which are needed:

   (a) To improve methods of production, conservation and distribution of food by making full use of technical and scientific knowledge, by disseminating knowledge of the principles of nutrition and by developing or reforming agrarian systems in such a way as to achieve the most efficient development and utilization of natural resources;

   (b) Taking into account the problems of both food-importing and food-exporting countries, to ensure an equitable distribution of world food supplies in relation to need.

Article 12

1. The States Parties to the present Covenant recognize the right of everyone to the enjoyment of the highest attainable standard of physical and mental health.

2. The steps to be taken by the States Parties to the present Covenant to achieve the full realization of this right shall include those necessary for:

(a) The provision for the reduction of the stillbirth-rate and of infant mortality and for the healthy development of the child;

(b) The improvement of all aspects of environmental and industrial hygiene;

(c) The prevention, treatment and control of epidemic, endemic, occupational and other diseases;

(d) The creation of conditions which would assure to all medical service and medical attention in the event of sickness.

Article 13

1. The States Parties to the present Covenant recognize the right of everyone to education. They agree that education shall be directed to the full development of the human personality and the sense of its dignity, and shall strengthen the respect for human rights and fundamental freedoms. They further agree that education shall enable all persons to participate effectively in a free society, promote understanding, tolerance and friendship among all nations and all racial, ethnic or religious groups, and further the activities of the United Nations for the maintenance of peace.

2. The States Parties to the present Covenant recognize that, with a view to achieving the full realization of this right:

   (a) Primary education shall be compulsory and available free to all;

   (b) Secondary education in its different forms, including technical and vocational secondary education, shall be made generally available and accessible to all by every appropriate means, and in particular by the progressive introduction of free education;

   (c) Higher education shall be made equally accessible to all, on the basis of capacity, by every appropriate means, and in particular by the progressive introduction of free education;

   (d) Fundamental education shall be encouraged or

intensified as far as possible for those persons who have not received or completed the whole period of their primary education;

(e) The development of a system of schools at all levels shall be actively pursued, an adequate fellowship system shall be established, and the material conditions of teaching staff shall be continuously improved.

3. The States Parties to the present Covenant undertake to have respect for the liberty of parents and, when applicable, legal guardians to choose for their children schools, other than those established by the public authorities, which conform to such minimum educational standards as may be laid down or approved by the State and to ensure the religious and moral education of their children in conformity with their own convictions.

4. No part of this article shall be construed so as to interfere with the liberty of individuals and bodies to establish and direct educational institutions, subject always to the observance of the principles set forth in paragraph I of this article and to the requirement that the education given in such institutions shall conform to such minimum standards as may be laid down by the State.

Article 14

Each State Party to the present Covenant which, at the time of becoming a Party, has not been able to secure in its metropolitan territory or other territories under its jurisdiction compulsory primary education, free of charge, undertakes, within two years, to work out and adopt a detailed plan of action for the progressive implementation, within a reasonable number of years, to be fixed in the plan, of the principle of compulsory education free of charge for all.

Article 15

1. The States Parties to the present Covenant recognize the right of everyone:

   (a) To take part in cultural life;

(b) To enjoy the benefits of scientific progress and its applications;

(c) To benefit from the protection of the moral and material interests resulting from any scientific, literary or artistic production of which he is the author.

2. The steps to be taken by the States Parties to the present Covenant to achieve the full realization of this right shall include those necessary for the conservation, the development and the diffusion of science and culture.

3. The States Parties to the present Covenant undertake to respect the freedom indispensable for scientific research and creative activity.

4. The States Parties to the present Covenant recognize the benefits to be derived from the encouragement and development of international contacts and co-operation in the scientific and cultural fields.

PART IV

Article 16

1. The States Parties to the present Covenant undertake to submit in conformity with this part of the Covenant reports on the measures which they have adopted and the progress made in achieving the observance of the rights recognized herein.

2. (a) All reports shall be submitted to the Secretary-General of the United Nations, who shall transmit copies to the Economic and Social Council for consideration in accordance with the provisions of the present Covenant;

(b) The Secretary-General of the United Nations shall also transmit to the specialized agencies copies of the reports, or any relevant parts therefrom, from States Parties to the present Covenant which are also members of these specialized agencies in so far as these reports, or parts therefrom, relate to any matters which fall within the responsibilities of the said agencies in accordance with their constitutional instruments.

Article 17

1. The States Parties to the present Covenant shall furnish their reports in stages, in accordance with a programme to be established by the Economic and Social Council within one year of the entry into force of the present Covenant after consultation with the States Parties and the specialized agencies concerned.
2. Reports may indicate factors and difficulties affecting the degree of fulfilment of obligations under the present Covenant.
3. Where relevant information has previously been furnished to the United Nations or to any specialized agency by any State Party to the present Covenant, it will not be necessary to reproduce that information, but a precise reference to the information so furnished will suffice.

Article 18

Pursuant to its responsibilities under the Charter of the United Nations in the field of human rights and fundamental freedoms, the Economic and Social Council may make arrangements with the specialized agencies in respect of their reporting to it on the progress made in achieving the observance of the provisions of the present Covenant falling within the scope of their activities. These reports may include particulars of decisions and recommendations on such implementation adopted by their competent organs.

Article 19

The Economic and Social Council may transmit to the Commission on Human Rights for study and general recommendation or, as appropriate, for information the reports concerning human rights submitted by States in accordance with articles 16 and 17, and those concerning human rights submitted by the specialized agencies in accordance with article 18.

Article 20

The States Parties to the present Covenant and the specialized agencies concerned may submit comments to the Economic and Social Council on any general recommendation under article 19 or reference to such general recommendation in any report of the Commission on Human Rights or any documentation referred to therein.

Article 21

The Economic and Social Council may submit from time to time to the General Assembly reports with recommendations of a general nature and a summary of the information received from the States Parties to the present Covenant and the specialized agencies on the measures taken and the progress made in achieving general observance of the rights recognized in the present Covenant.

Article 22

The Economic and Social Council may bring to the attention of other organs of the United Nations, their subsidiary organs and specialized agencies concerned with furnishing technical assistance any matters arising out of the reports referred to in this part of the present Covenant which may assist such bodies in deciding, each within its field of competence, on the advisability of international measures likely to contribute to the effective progressive implementation of the present Covenant.

Article 23

The States Parties to the present Covenant agree that international action for the achievement of the rights recognized in the present Covenant includes such methods as the conclusion of conventions, the adoption of recommendations, the furnishing of technical assistance and the holding of regional meetings and technical meetings for the purpose of consultation and study organized in conjunction with the Governments concerned.

Article 24

Nothing in the present Covenant shall be interpreted as impairing the provisions of the Charter of the United Nations and of the constitutions of the specialized agencies which define the respective responsibilities of the various organs of the United Nations and of the specialized agencies in regard to the matters dealt with in the present Covenant.

Article 25

Nothing in the present Covenant shall be interpreted as impairing the inherent right of all peoples to enjoy and utilize fully and freely their natural wealth and resources.

PART V

Article 26

1. The present Covenant is open for signature by any State Member of the United Nations or member of any of its specialized agencies, by any State Party to the Statute of the International Court of Justice, and by any other State which has been invited by the General Assembly of the United Nations to become a party to the present Covenant.

2. The present Covenant is subject to ratification. Instruments of ratification shall be deposited with the Secretary-General of the United Nations.

3. The present Covenant shall be open to accession by any State referred to in paragraph 1 of this article.

4. Accession shall be effected by the deposit of an instrument of accession with the Secretary-General of the United Nations.

5. The Secretary-General of the United Nations shall inform all States which have signed the present Covenant or acceded to it of the deposit of each instrument of ratification or accession.

Article 27

1. The present Covenant shall enter into force three months after the date of the deposit with the Secretary-General of the United Nations of the thirty-fifth instrument of ratification or instrument of accession.

2. For each State ratifying the present Covenant or acceding to it after the deposit of the thirty-fifth instrument of ratification or instrument of accession, the present Covenant shall enter into force three months after the date of the deposit of its own instrument of ratification or instrument of accession.

Article 28

The provisions of the present Covenant shall extend to all parts of federal States without any limitations or exceptions.

Article 29

1. Any State Party to the present Covenant may propose an amendment and file it with the Secretary-General of the United Nations. The Secretary-General shall thereupon communicate any proposed amendments to the States Parties to the present Covenant with a request that they notify him whether they favour a conference of States Parties for the purpose of considering and voting upon the proposals. In the event that at least one third of the States Parties favours such a conference, the Secretary-General shall convene the conference under the auspices of the United Nations. Any amendment adopted by a majority of the States Parties present and voting at the conference shall be submitted to the General Assembly of the United Nations for approval.
2. Amendments shall come into force when they have been approved by the General Assembly of the United Nations and accepted by a two-thirds majority of the States Parties to the present Covenant in accordance with their respective constitutional processes.
3. When amendments come into force they shall be binding on those States Parties which have accepted them, other States Parties still being bound by the provisions of the present Covenant and any earlier amendment which they have accepted.

Article 30

Irrespective of the notifications made under article 26, paragraph 5, the Secretary-General of the United Nations shall inform all States referred to in paragraph I of the same article of the following particulars:

(a) Signatures, ratifications and accessions under article 26;

(b) The date of the entry into force of the present Covenant under article 27 and the date of the entry into force of any amendments under article 29.

Article 31

1. The present Covenant, of which the Chinese, English, French, Russian and Spanish texts are equally authentic, shall be deposited in the archives of the United Nations.
2. The Secretary-General of the United Nations shall transmit certified copies of the present Covenant to all States referred to in article 26.

APPENDIX VII

THE PROTECTION OF HUMAN RIGHTS ACT, 1993*

The Protection of Human Rights Act, 1993 [As amended by the Protection of Human Rights (Amendment) Act, 2006–No. 43 of 2006]

No. 10 of 1994

(8th January, 1994)

An Act to provide for the constitution of a National Human Rights Commission, State Human Rights Commission in States and Human Rights Courts for better protection of human rights and for matters connected therewith or incidental there to.

Be it enacted by Parliament in the forty-fourth year of the Republic of India as follows:

CHAPTER I

PRELIMINARY

1. Short title, extent and commencement

(1) This Act may be called the Protection of Human Rights Act, 1993.**

(2) It extends to the whole of India. Provided that it shall apply to the State of Jammu and Kashmir only in so far as it pertains to the matters relatable to any of the entries enumerated in List I or List lll in the Seventh Schedule to the Constitution as applicable to that State.

(3) It shall be deemed to have come into force on the 28th day of September, 1993.

2. Definitions

(1) In this Act, unless the context otherwise requires-

---

* As amended by the Protection of Human Rights (Amendment) Act, 2006– No. 43 of 2006.

** Amended vide Protection of Human Rights (Amendment) Act, 2006 (No. 43 of 2006).

(a) "armed forces" means the naval, military and air forces and includes any other armed forces of the Union;

(b) "Chairperson" means the Chairperson of the Commission or of the State Commission, as the case may be;

(c) "Commission" means the National Human Rights Commission under section 3;

(d) "human rights" means the rights relating to life, liberty, equality and dignity of the individual guaranteed by the Constitution or embodied in the International Covenants and enforceable by courts in India.

(e) "Human Rights Court" means the Human Rights Court specified under section 30;

(f) "International Covenants" means the International Covenant on Civil and Political Rights and the International Covenant on Economic, Social and Cultural rights adopted by the General Assembly of the United Nations on the 16th 1

December, 1966 [and such other Covenant or Convention adopted by the General Assembly of the United Nations as the Central Government may, by notification, specify"][1];

(g) "Member" means a Member of the Commission or of the State Commission, as the case may be[2];

(h) "National Commission for Minorities" means the National Commission for Minorities constituted under section 3 of the National Commission for Minorities Act, 1992;

(i) "National Commission for the Scheduled Castes" means the National Commission for the Scheduled Castes referred to in Article 338 of the Constitution[1];

(ia) "National Commission for the Scheduled Tribes" means the National Commission for the Scheduled Tribes referred to in Article 338A of the Constitution[2];

---

1 Added by Act 43 of 2006

2 Subs. by Act 43 of 2006

(j) "National Commission for Women" means the National Commission for Women constituted under section 3 of the National Commission for Women Act, 1990;

(k) "Notification" means a notification published in the official Gazette;

(l) "Prescribed" means prescribed by rules made under this Act;

(m) "Public servant" shall have the meaning assigned to it in section 21 of the Indian Penal Code;

(n) "State Commission" means a State Human Rights Commission constituted under section 21.

(2) Any reference in this Act to a law, which is not in force in the State of Jammu and Kashmir, shall, in relation to that State, be construed as a reference to a corresponding law, if any, in force in that State.

CHAPTER II

THE NATIONAL HUMAN RIGHTS COMMISSION

3. Constitution of a National Human Rights Commission

(1) The Central Government shall constitute a body to be known as the National Human Rights Commission to exercise the powers conferred upon, and to perform the functions assigned to it, under this Act.

(2) The Commission shall consist of:

(a) a Chairperson who has been a Chief Justice of the Supreme Court;

(b) one Member who is or has been, a Judge of the Supreme Court;

(c) one Member who is, or has been, the Chief Justice of a High Court;

(d) two Members to be appointed from amongst persons having knowledge of, or practical experience in, matters relating to human rights.

(3) The Chairperson of the National Commission for Minorities,

1[the National Commission for the Scheduled Castes, the National Commission for the Scheduled Tribes] and the National Commission for Women shall be deemed to be Members of the Commission for the discharge of functions specified in clauses (b) to (j) of section 12.

(4) There shall be a Secretary-General who shall be the Chief Executive Officer of the Commission and shall exercise such powers and discharge such functions of the Commission2 [except judicial functions and the power to make regulations under section 40 B], as may be delegated to him by the Commission or the Chairperson as the case may be. 1 Subs. by Act 43 of 2006 for "The National Commission for the Scheduled Castes and Scheduled Tribes." 2 Subs. by Act 43 of 2006 for "as it may delegate to him."

President may, by notification, authorise one of the Members to act as the Chairperson until the appointment of a new Chairperson to fill such vacancy.

(2) When the Chairperson is unable to discharge his functions owing to absence on leave or otherwise, such one of the Members as the President may, by notification, authorise in this behalf, shall discharge the functions of the Chairperson until the date on which the Chairperson resumes his duties.

8. Terms and conditions of service of Chairperson and Members

The salaries and allowances payable to, and other terms and conditions of service of, the[1] [Chairperson and] Members shall be such as may be prescribed. Provided that neither the salary and allowances nor the other terms and conditions of service of[2] [the Chairperson or] a Member shall be varied to his disadvantage after his appointment.]

---

1. Inserted by Act 43 of 2006
2. Inserted by Act 43 of 2006
3. Subs. by Act 43 of 2006

9. Vacancies, etc., not to invalidate the proceedings of the Commission

No act or proceedings of the Commission shall be questioned or shall be invalidated merely on the ground of existence of any vacancy or defect in the constitution of the Commission.

10. Procedure to be regulated by the Commission

(1) The Commission shall meet at such time and place as the Chairperson may think fit.

(2) Subject to the provisions of this Act and the rules made there under, the Commission shall have the power to lay down by regulations

(3) All orders and decisions of the Commission shall be authenticated by the Secretary-General or any other officer of the Commission duly authorised by the Chairperson in this behalf.

11. Officers and other staff of the Commission

(1) The Central Government shall make available to the Commission:

 (a) an officer of the rank of the Secretary to the Government of India who shall be the Secretary-General of the Commission; and

 (b) such police and investigative staff under an officer not below the rank of a Director General of Police and such other officers and staff as may be necessary for the efficient performance of the functions of the Commission.

(2) Subject to such rules as may be made by the Central Government in this behalf, the Commission may appoint such other administrative, technical and scientific staff as it may consider necessary.

(3) The salaries, allowances and conditions of service of the officers and other staff appointed under sub-section (2) shall be such as may be prescribed.

CHAPTER III

FUNCTIONS AND POWERS OF THE COMMISSION

12. Functions of the Commission

The Commission shall perform all or any of the following functions, namely:-

(a) inquire, suo motu or on a petition presented to it by a victim or any person on his behalf [or on a direction or order of any court][1], into complaint of

(i) violation of human rights or abetment thereof; or

(ii) negligence in the prevention of such violation, by a public servant;

(b) intervene in any proceeding involving any allegation of violation of human rights pending before a court with the approval of such court;[2]

(c) visit, notwithstanding anything contained in any other law for the time being in force, any jail or other institution under the control of the State Government, where persons are detained or lodged for purposes of treatment, reformation or protection, for the study of the living conditions of the inmates thereof and make recommendations thereon to the Government;

(d) review the safeguards provided by or under the Constitution or any law for the time being in force for the protection of human rights and recommend measures for their effective implementation;

(e) review the factors, including acts of terrorism that inhibit the enjoyment of human rights and recommend appropriate remedial.

(f) study treaties and other international instruments on human rights and make recommendations for their effective implementation;

1. Inserted by Act 43 of 2006
2. Sub. by Act 43 of 2006

(g) undertake and promote research in the field of human rights;

(h) spread human rights literacy among various sections of society and promote awareness of the safeguards available for the protection of these rights through publications, the media, seminars and other available means;

(i) encourage the efforts of non-governmental organisations and institutions working in the field of human rights;

(j) such other functions as it may consider necessary for the protection of human rights.

13. Powers relating to Inquiries

(1) The Commission shall, while inquiring into complaints under this Act, have all the powers of a civil court trying a suit under the Code of Civil Procedure, 1908, and in particular in respect of the following matters, namely:

(a) summoning and enforcing the attendance of witnesses and examining them on oath;

(b) discovery and production of any document;

(c) receiving evidence on affidavits;

(d) requisitioning any public record or copy thereof from any court or office;

(e) issuing commissions for the examination of witnesses or documents;

(f) any other matter which may be prescribed.

(2) The Commission shall have power to require any person, subject to any privilege which may be claimed by that person under any law for the time being in force, to furnish information on such points or matters as, in the opinion of the Commission, may be useful for, or relevant to, the subject matter of the inquiry and any person so required shall be deemed to be legally bound to furnish such information within the meaning of section 176 and section 177 of the Indian Penal Code.

(3) The Commission or any other officer, not below the rank of a Gazetted Officer, specially authorised in this behalf by the

Commission may enter any building or place where the Commission has reason to believe that any document relating to the subject matter of the inquiry may be found, and may seize any such document or take extracts or copies there from subject to the provisions of section 100 of the Code of Criminal Procedure, 1973, in so far as it may be applicable.

(4) The Commission shall be deemed to be a civil court and when any offence as is described in section 175, section 178, section 179, section 180 or section 228 of the Indian Penal Code is committed in the view or presence of the Commission, the Commission may, after recording the facts constituting the offence and the statement of the accused as provided for in the Code of Criminal Procedure, 1973, forward the case to a Magistrate having jurisdiction to try the same and the Magistrate to whom any such case is forwarded shall proceed to hear the complaint against the accused as if the case has been forwarded to him under section 346 of the Code of Criminal Procedure, 1973.

(5) Every proceeding before the Commission shall be deemed to be a judicial proceeding within the meaning of sections 193 and 228, and for the purposes of section 196, of the Indian Penal Code, and the Commission shall be deemed to be a civil court for all the purposes of section 195 and Chapter XXVI of the Code of Criminal Procedure, 1973.

(6)1 Where the Commission considers it necessary or expedient so to do, it may, by order, transfer any complaint filed or pending before it to the State Commission of the State from which the complaint arises, for disposal in accordance with the provisions of this Act; Provided that no such complaint shall be transferred unless the same is one respecting which the State Commission has jurisdiction to entertain the same.

(7)1 Every complaint transferred under sub-section(6) shall be dealt with and disposed of by the State Commission as if it were a complaint initially filed before it.

---

1 Inserted by Act 43 of 2006

14. Investigation

(1) The Commission may, for the purpose of conducting any investigation pertaining to the inquiry, utilise the services of any officer or investigation agency of the Central Government or any State Government with the concurrence of the Central Government or the State Government, as the case may be.

(2) For the purpose of investigating into any matter pertaining to the inquiry, any officer or agency whose services are utilised under subsection

(1) may, subject to the direction and control of the Commission:-

   (a) summon and enforce the attendance of any person and examine him;

   (b) require the discovery and production of any document; and

   (c) requisition any public record or copy thereof from any office.

(3) The provisions of section 15 shall apply in relation to any statement made by a person before any officer or agency whose services are utilised under sub-section (1) as they apply in relation to any statement made by a person in the course of giving evidence before the Commission.

(4) The officer or agency whose services are utilised under subsection (1) shall investigate into any matter pertaining to the inquiry and submit a report thereon to the Commission within such period as may be specified by the Commission in this behalf.

(5) The Commission shall satisfy itself about the correctness of the facts stated and the conclusion, if any, arrived at in the report submitted to it under sub-section

(4) and for this purpose the Commission may make such inquiry (including the examination of the person or persons who conducted or assisted in the investigation) as it thinks fit.

---

1 Inserted by Act 43 of 2006 or to the victim or the members of his family as the Commission may consider necessary;

(ii) to initiate proceedings for prosecution or such other suitable action as the Commission may deem fit against the concerned person or persons;

(iii) to take such further action as it may think fit;

(b) approach the Supreme Court or the High Court concerned for such directions, orders or writs as that Court may deem necessary;

(c) recommend to the concerned Government or authority at any stage of the inquiry for the grant of such immediate interim relief to the victim or the members of his family as the Commission may consider necessary;

(d) s ubject to the provisions of clause

(e) provide a copy of the inquiry report to the petitioner or his representative;

(e) the Commission shall send a copy of its inquiry report together with its recommendations to the concerned Government or authority and the concerned Government or authority shall, within a period of one month, or such further time as the Commission may allow, forward its comments on the report, including the action taken or proposed to be taken thereon, to the Commission;

(f) the Commission shall publish its inquiry report together with the comments of the concerned Government or authority, if any, and the action taken or proposed to be taken by the concerned Government or authority on the recommendations of the Commission.][1]

19. Procedure with respect to armed forces

(1) Notwithstanding anything contained in this Act, while dealing with complaints of violation of human rights by members of the armed forces, the Commission shall adopt the following procedure, namely :-

(a) it may, either on its own motion or on receipt of a petition, seek a report from the Central Government;

---

1 Subs. by Act 43 of 2006

(b) after the receipt of the report, it may, either not proceed with the complaint or, as the case may be, make its recommendations to that Government.

(2) The Central Government shall inform the Commission of the action taken on the recommendations within three months or such further time as the Commission may allow.

(3) The Commission shall publish its report together with its recommendations made to the Central Government and the action taken by that Government on such recommendations.

(4) The Commission shall provide a copy of the report published under sub-section (3) to the petitioner or his representative.

20. Annual and special reports of the Commission

(1) The Commission shall submit an annual report to the Central Government and to the State Government concerned and may at any time submit special reports on any matter which, in its opinion, is of such urgency or importance that it should not be deferred till submission of the annual report.

(2) The Central Government and the State Government, as the case may be, shall cause the annual and special reports of the Commission to be laid before each House of Parliament or the State Legislature respectively, as the case may be, along with a memorandum of action taken or proposed to be taken on the recommendations of the Commission and the reasons for non-acceptance of the recommendations, if any.

CHAPTER V

STATE HUMAN RIGHTS COMMISSIONS

21. Constitution of State Human Rights Commissions

(1) A State Government may constitute a body to be known as the .... (name of the State) Human Rights Commission to exercise the powers conferred upon, and to perform the functions assigned to, a State Commission under this chapter.

(2)1 [The State Commission shall, with effect from such date as the State Government may by notification specify, consist of—

(a) a Chairperson who has been a Chief Justice of a High Court;

(b) one Member who is, or has been, a Judge of a High Court or District Judge in the State with a minimum of seven years experience as District Judge;

(c) one Member to be appointed from amongst persons having knowledge of, or practical experience in, matters relating to human rights.][1]

(3) There shall be a Secretary who shall be the Chief Executive Officer of the State Commission and shall exercise such powers and discharge such functions of the State Commission as it may delegate to him.

(4) The headquarters of the State Commission shall be at such place as the State Government may, by notification, specify.

(5) A State Commission may inquire into violation of human rights only in respect of matters relatable to any of the entries enumerated in List II and List III in the Seventh Schedule to the Constitution:

Provided that if any such matter is already being inquired into by the Commission or any other Commission duly constituted under any law for the time being in force, the State Commission shall not inquire into the said matter:

Provided further that in relation to the Jammu and Kashmir Human Rights Commission, this sub-section shall have effect as if for the words and figures "List II and List III in the Seventh Schedule to the Constitution", the words and figures "List III in the Seventh Schedule to the Constitution as applicable to the State of Jammu and Kashmir and in respect of matters in relation to which the Legislature of that State has power to make laws" had been substituted.

(6) [Two or more State Governments may, with the consent of a Chairperson or Member of a State Commission, appoint such Chairperson or, as the case may be, such Member of another State

---

1 Subs. by Act 43 of 2006

Commission simultaneously if such Chairperson or Member consents to such appointment:

Provided that every appointment made under this sub-section shall be made after obtaining the recommendations of the Committee referred to in sub-section(1) of section 22 in respect of the State for which a common Chairperson or Member, or both, as the case may be, is to be appointed.][1]

22. Appointment of Chairperson and [Members]2 of State Commission

(1) The Chairperson and [Members][2] shall be appointed by the Governor by warrant under his hand and seal: Provided that every appointment under this sub-section shall be made after obtaining the recommendation of a Committee consisting of

(a) the Chief Minister — Chairperson

(b) Speaker of the Legislative Assembly — Member

(c) Minister in-charge of the Department of Home, in that State — Member

(d) Leader of the Opposition in the Legislative Assembly — Member Provided further that where there is a Legislative Council in a State, the Chairman of that Council and the Leader of the Opposition in that Council shall also be members of the Committee. Provided also that no sitting Judge of a High Court or a sitting District Judge shall be appointed except after consultation with the Chief Justice of the High Court of the concerned State.

(2) No appointment of a Chairperson or a Member of the State Commission shall be invalid merely by reason of [any vacancy of any Member in the Committee referred to in sub-section(1)].[3]

---

1. Subs. by Act 43 of 2006
2. Subs. by Act 43 of 2006 for "other Members"
3. Subs. by Act 43 of 2006 for "any vacancy in the Committee"

23. [Resignation and Removal of Chairperson or a Member of the State Commission][1]

[2][(1) The Chairperson or a Member of a State Commission may, by notice in writing under his hand addressed to the Governor, resign his office (1A) Subject to the provisions of sub-section (2), the Chairperson or any Member of the State Commission shall only be removed from his office by order of the President on the ground of proved misbehavior or incapacity after the Supreme Court, on a reference being made to it by the President, has, on inquiry held in accordance with the procedure prescribed in that behalf by the Supreme Court, reported that the Chairperson or such Member, as the case may be, ought on any such ground to be removed.]

(2) Notwithstanding anything in sub-section (1A), the President may by order remove from office the Chairperson or any [Member][3] if the Chairperson or such [Member][4], as the case may be –

(a) is adjudged an insolvent; or

(b) engages during his term of office in any paid employment outside the duties of his office; or

(c) is unfit to continue in office by reason of infirmity of mind or body; or

(d) is of unsound mind and stands so declared by a competent court; or

(e) i s convicted and sentenced to imprisonment for an offence which in the opinion of the President involves moral turpitude.

---

1. Subs. by Act 43 of 2006 for "Removal of a member of the State Commission
2. Subs. by Act 43 of 2006
3. Subs. by Act 43 of 2006 for "other member"
4. Subs. by Act 43 of 2006 for "other member"

24. Term of office of [Chairperson and][1] Members of the State Commission

(1) A person appointed as Chairperson shall hold office for a term of five years from the date on which he enters upon his office or until he attains the age of seventy years, whichever is earlier;

(2) A person appointed as a Member shall hold office for a term of five years from the date on which he enters upon his office and shall be eligible for re-appointment for another term of five years; Provided that no Member shall hold office after he has attained the age of seventy years.

(3) On ceasing to hold office, a Chairperson or a Member shall be ineligible for further employment under the Government of a State or under the Government of India.

25. Member to act as Chairperson or to discharge his functions in certain circumstances

(1) In the event of the occurrence of any vacancy in the office of the Chairperson by reason of his death, resignation or otherwise, the Governor may, by notification, authorise one of the Members to act as the Chairperson until the appointment of a new Chairperson to fill such vacancy.

(2) When the Chairperson is unable to discharge his functions owing to absence on leave or otherwise, such one of the Members as the Governor may, by notification, authorise in this behalf, shall discharge the functions of the Chairperson until the date on which the Chairperson resumes his duties.

26. [Terms and conditions of service of Chairperson and Members of the State Commissions

The salaries and allowances payable to, and other terms and conditions of service of, the Chairperson and Members shall be such as may be prescribed by the State Government; Provided that neither the salary and allowances nor the other terms and conditions of service of the Chairperson or a Member shall be varied to his disadvantage after his appointment.][2]

---

1. Inserted by Act 43 of 2006
2. Subs. by Act 43 of 2006

27. Officers and other staff of the State Commission

(1) The State Government shall make available to the Commission

(a) an officer not below the rank of a Secretary to the State Government who shall be the Secretary of the State Commission; and

(b) such police and investigative staff under an officer not below the rank of an Inspector General of Police and such other officers and staff as may be necessary for the efficient performance of the functions of the State Commission.

(2) subject to such rules as may be made by the State Government in this behalf, the State Commission may appoint such other administrative, technical and scientific staff as it may consider necessary.

(3) The salaries, allowances and conditions of service of the officers and other staff appointed under sub-section (2) shall be such as may be prescribed by the State Government.

28. Annual and special reports of State Commission

(1) The State Commission shall submit an annual report to the State Government and may at any time submit special reports on any matter which, in its opinion, is of such urgency or importance that it should not be deferred till submission of the annual report.

(2) The State Government shall cause the annual and special reports of the State Commission to be laid before each House of State Legislature where it consists of two Houses, or where such Legislature consists of one House, before that House along with a memorandum of action taken or proposed to be taken on the recommendations of the State Commission and the reasons for non-acceptance of the recommendations, if any.

29. Application of certain provisions relating to National Human Rights Commission to State Commissions

The provisions of sections 9, 10, 12, 13, 14, 15, 16, 17 and 18 shall apply to a State Commission and shall have effect, subject to the following modifications, namely:-

(a) references to "Commission" shall be construed as references to "State Commission";

(b) in section 10, in sub-section (3), for the word "Secretary General", the word "Secretary" shall be substituted;

(c) in section 12, clause (f) shall be omitted;

(d) in section 17, in clause (i), the words "Central Government or any" shall be omitted;

CHAPTER VI

HUMAN RIGHTS COURTS

30. For the purpose of providing speedy trial of offences arising out of violation of human rights, the State Government may, with the concurrence of the Chief Justice of the High Court, by notification, specify for each district a Court of Session to be a Human Rights Court to try the said offences. Provided that nothing in this section shall apply if

(a) a Court of Session is already specified as a special court; or

(b) a special court is already constituted, for such offences under any other law for the time being in force.

31. Special Public Prosecutor

For every Human Rights Court, the State Government shall, by notification, specify a Public Prosecutor or appoint an advocate who has been in practice as an advocate for not less than seven years, as a Special Public Prosecutor for the purpose of conducting cases in that Court.

CHAPTER VII

FINANCE, ACCOUNTS AND AUDIT

32. Grants by the Central Government

(1) The Central Government shall after due appropriation made by Parliament by law in this behalf, pay to the Commission by way of grants such sums of money as the Central Government may think fit for being utilised for the purposes of this Act.

(2) The Commission may spend such sums as it thinks fit for performing the functions under this Act, and such sums shall be treated as expenditure payable out of the grants referred to in sub-section (1).

33. Grants by the State Government

(1) The State Government shall, after due appropriation made by Legislature by law in this behalf, pay to the State Commission by way of grants such sums of money as the State Government may think fit for being utilised for the purposes of this Act.

(2) The State Commission may spend such sums as it thinks fit for performing the functions under Chapter V, and such sums shall be treated as expenditure payable out of the grants referred to in sub-section (1).

34. Accounts and Audit

(1) The Commission shall maintain proper accounts and other relevant records and prepare an annual statement of accounts in such form as may be prescribed by the Central Government in consultation with the Comptroller and Auditor-General of India.

(2) The Accounts of the Commission shall be audited by the Comptroller and Auditor-General at such intervals as may be specified by him and any expenditure incurred in connection with such audit shall be payable by the Commission to the Comptroller and Auditor-General.

(3) The Comptroller and Auditor-General or any person appointed by him in connection with the audit of the accounts of the Commission under this Act shall have the same rights and privileges and the authority in connection with such audit as the Comptroller and Auditor-General generally has in connection with the audit of Government accounts and, in particular, shall have the right to demand the production of books, accounts, connected vouchers and other documents and papers and to inspect any of the offices of the Commission.

(4) The accounts of the Commission as certified by the Comptroller and Auditor-General or any other person appointed by him in this behalf, together with the audit report thereon shall

be forwarded annually to the Central Government by the Commission and the Central Government shall cause the audit report to be laid as soon as may be after it is received before each House of Parliament.

35. Accounts and Audit of State Commission

(1) The State Commission shall maintain proper accounts and other relevant records and prepare an annual statement of accounts in such form as may be prescribed by the State Government in consultation with the Comptroller and Auditor-General of India.

(2) The accounts of the State Commission shall be audited by the Comptroller and Auditor-General at such intervals as may be specified by him and any expenditure incurred in connection with such audit shall be payable by the State Commission to the Comptroller and Auditor-General.

(3) The Comptroller and Auditor-General or any person appointed by him in connection with the audit of the accounts of the State Commission under this Act shall have the same rights and privileges and the authority in connection with such audit as the Comptroller and Auditor-General generally has in connection with the audit of Government accounts and, in particular, shall have the right to demand the production of books, accounts, connected vouchers and other documents and papers and to inspect any of the offices of the State Commission.

(4) The accounts of the State Commission, as certified by the Comptroller and Auditor-General or any other person appointed by him in this behalf, together with the audit report thereon, shall be forwarded annually to the State Government by the State Commission and the State Government shall cause the audit report to be laid, as soon as may be after it is received, before the State Legislature.

CHAPTER VIII

MISCELLANEOUS

36. Matters not subject to jurisdiction of the Commission

(1) The Commission shall not inquire into any matter which

is pending before a State Commission or any other Commission duly constituted under any law for the time being in force.

(2) The Commission or the State Commission shall not inquire into any matter after the expiry of one year from the date on which the act constituting violation of human rights is alleged to have been committed.

37. Constitution of Special Investigation Teams

Notwithstanding anything contained in any other law for the time being in force, where the Government considers it necessary so to do, it may constitute one or more special investigation teams, consisting of such police officers as it thinks necessary for purposes of investigation and prosecution of offences arising out of violations of human rights.

38. Protection of action taken in good faith

No suit or other legal proceeding shall lie against the Central Government, State Government, Commission, the State Commission or any Member thereof or any person acting under the direction either of the Central Government, State Government, Commission or the State Commission in respect of anything which is in good faith done or intended to be done in pursuance of this Act or of any rules or any order made there under or in respect of the publication by or under the authority of the Central Government, State Government, Commission or the State Commission of any report paper or proceedings.

39. Members and officers to be public servants

Every Member of the Commission, State Commission and every officer appointed or authorised by the Commission or the State Commission to exercise functions under this Act shall be deemed to be a public servant within the meaning of section 21 of the Indian Penal Code.

40. Power of Central Government to make rules

(1) The Central Government may, by notification, make rules to carry out the provisions of this Act.

(2) In particular and without prejudice to the generality of the foregoing power, such rules may provide for all or any of the following matters namely :-

(a) the salaries and allowances and other terms and conditions of service of the [Chairperson and Members][1] under section 8;

(b) the conditions subject to which other administrative, technical and scientific staff may be appointed by the Commission and the salaries and allowances of officers and other staff under subsection

(3) of section 11;

(c) any other power of a civil court required to be prescribed under clause

(d) the form in which the annual statement of accounts is to be prepared by the Commission under sub-section (1) of section 34; and

(e) any other matter which has to be, or may be, prescribed.

(f) of sub-section (1) of section 13;

(3) Every rule made under this Act shall be laid, as soon as may be after it is made, before each House of Parliament, while it is in session, for a total period of thirty days which may be comprised in one session or in two or more successive sessions, and if, before the expiry of the session immediately following the session or the successive sessions aforesaid, both Houses agree in making any modification in the rule or both Houses agree that the rule should not be made, the rule shall thereafter have effect only in such modified form or be of no effect, as the case may be; so however, that any such modification or annulment shall be without prejudice to the validity of anything previously done under that rule.

40 A. Power to make rules retrospectively—

The power to make rules under clause (b) of sub-section (2) of section 40 shall include the power to make such rules or any of them retrospectively from a date not earlier than the date on which this Act received the assent of the President, but no such retrospective effect shall be given to any such rule so as to

1. Subs. by Act 43 of 2006 for "members"

prejudicially affect the interests of any person to whom such rule may be applicable.

Power of Commission to make Regulations[1]

[2][**40(B)** (1) Subject to the provisions of this Act and the rules made there under, the Commission may, with the previous approval of the Central Government, by notification, make regulations to carry out the provisions of this Act.

(2) In particular and without prejudice to the generality of the foregoing power, such regulations may provide for all or any of the following matters, namely:-

(a) the procedure to be followed by the Commission under subsection(2) of Section 10;

(b) the returns and statistics to be furnished by the State Commission;

(c) any other matter which has to be, or may be, specified by regulations.

(3) Every regulation made by the Commission under this Act shall be laid, as soon as may be after it is made, before each House of Parliament, while it is in session, for a total period of thirty days which may be comprised in one session or in two or more successive sessions, and if, before the expiry of the session or the successive sessions aforesaid, both Houses agree in making any modification in the regulations or both Houses agree that the regulation should not be made, the regulation shall thereafter have effect only in such modified form or be of no effect, as the case may be; so however, that any such modification or annulment shall be without prejudice to the validity of anything previously done under that regulation.]

41. Power of State Government to make rules

(1) The State Government may, by notification, make rules to carry out the provisions of this Act.

---

1. Inserted by Act 43 of 2006
2. Inserted by Act 43 of 2006

(2) In particular and without prejudice to the generality of the foregoing power, such rules may provide for all or any of the following matters, namely :

(a) the salaries and allowances and other terms and conditions of service of the Chairperson and Members under section 26;

(b) the conditions subject to which other administrative, technical and scientific staff may be appointed by the State Commission and the salaries and allowances of officers and other staff under sub-section (3) of section 27;

(c) the form in which the annual statement of accounts is to be prepared under sub-section (1) of section 35.

(3) Every rule made by the State Government under this section shall be laid, as soon as may be after it is made, before each House of the State Legislature where it consists of two Houses, or where such Legislature consists of one House, before that House.

42. Power to remove Difficulties

(1) If any difficulty arises in giving effect to the provisions of this Act, the Central Government, may by order published in the Official Gazette, make such provisions, not inconsistent with the provisions of this Act as appear to it to be necessary or expedient for removing the difficulty. Provided that no such order shall be made after the expiry of the period of two years from the date of commencement of this Act.

(2) Every order made under this section shall, as soon as may be after it is made, be laid before each house of Parliament.

43. Repeal and Savings

(1) The Protection of Human Rights Ordinance, 1993 is hereby repealed.

(2) Notwithstanding such repeal, anything done or any action taken under the said Ordinance, shall be deemed to have been done or taken under the corresponding provisions of this Act.

Index

□□□